THE NEW REAL ESTATE
AGENT'S HANDBOOK

A Beginner's Guide to Getting Your First Sale and Achieving Long-Term Success & Proven Marketing & Sales Strategies for Building a Thriving Career As A Realtor

Nick Tsai

BONUSES

Thanks for getting this book; here are some resources to help you bring your real estate career to the next level.

Bonus 1- A 14 Days Free Trial Of Our Membership

You can also join our pro membership to get access to over 1700+ real estate marketing tools & templates for only a few bucks a day.

Go to https://soldouthouses.com/pro/ to try it for free.

Bonus 2- The Ultimate Real Estate Marketing Checklist

This checklist features 86 marketing tips to
generate more leads online & offline.

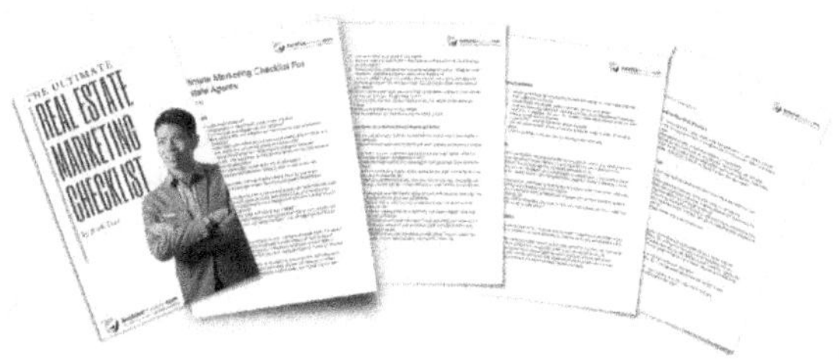

Download your free checklist at
https://soldouthouses.com/checklist

TABLE OF CONTENTS

INTRODUCTION

Thanks for getting the book.

You made a smart decision because, in this book, you will discover tips and strategies to grow your real estate business and success as a real estate agent.

If you have been in the real estate industry for a while, you know how competitive it is. And to stand out in the crowd, you must be extraordinary in every aspect of your marketing and selling.

Luckily, you don't have to fight alone. I published this book and founded Soldouthouses.com to help real estate professionals generate more leads and close sales.

The real estate market is a playground that many people want to dip their toe into because they see all of the possible money and potential in growing rich quickly. However, many don't realize that when entering into the real estate market they are entering into a high stakes, high risk industry that does have great payoffs, but can easily knock you down as quickly as it built you up.

One of the main reasons that people fail in real estate is that they don't understand the core basics and what it takes to succeed. Many believe that if they simply find a property, do some repairs and do a flip, they will make millions and millions of dollars.

In the early days of real estate, this may have been the case. However, with new technology, the decreased locations for new builds and with education and misinformation being spread like wildfire, people are holding on to their properties longer and wanting more money for what they have. In the early 1980's a house could be purchased for twenty thousand dollars. Today, the cheapest house you can find that is worth living in is almost three hundred and fifty thousand dollars in the bad neighborhoods.

This is the reason that I wrote this book. It is a simple guide that will walk you through the basics of what is involved getting into real estate. Now, this won't give you all the answers, tips and tricks and golden nuggets, what it will do is give you a collection of information and resources that I have gathered over the last several years of writing my blog, dealing with people interested in real estate and much more.

After completing this book, I want you to walk away with a better understanding of what is involved and then start to explore more on your own. Use this book as a guide to finding your own answers and if you do decide that you want to dive in and start getting involved with real estate, you will do it with a greater mindset.

To your success and let's dive in.

Who Am I?

Hi, my name is Nick Tsai. I'm a digital marketing expert, and I have over 10 years of marketing experience.

Ten years ago, I was a realtor. As a rookie, I struggled to get clients even though I followed the traditional advice from the industry:

- Distributing flyers
- Posting classified ads
- Cold calling
- Cold mailing

But nothing worked for me.

I was frustrated, tired of struggling, and hopeless. I worked 12-hour days, every day and still got no clients. I eventually burned out and quit. I lost my confidence and self-doubt crept in.

Those were the worst days of my life.

Then one day, I received a phone call that changed everything.

It was from a stranger who wanted me to help him sell this house.

I had never called him, never mailed him, and didn't even know who he was.

But, for some reason, he found my website.

It was an ugly blog I used as a personal notebook where I wrote down everything I learned about real estate.

For some strange reason, it became the #1 ranking real estate blog in my local area.

In the next few months, people kept calling. They asked me questions about real estate and even begged to be taken on as clients.

All of a sudden, I became the go-to expert in the local area.

And getting clients became effortless.

It was an "aha" moment for me and

I realized, "It's easier to attract clients than to chase clients."

In the past, I pursued potential clients by cold calling, cold mailing, and sending flyers (aka junk mail). I became an annoying salesperson.

But by harnessing the power of the internet, I can easily reach people who are ready to buy and can position myself as an expert!

So, I decided to dive into internet marketing to discover how I could attract more clients online. I studied countless marketing books, attended marketing seminars, and learned from the best marketing experts in the world.

And that's why I set up Soldouthouses.com so realtors like I once was can get results with digital marketing.

Be sure to visit https://Soldouthouses.com and discover all the real estate marketing tools & templates and follow our YouTube channel at https://youtube.com/@soldouthouses

CHAPTER ONE

THE BEGINNING OF YOUR JOURNEY

One of the biggest mistakes someone can make is diving into real estate or any other opportunity without starting from the beginning and learning the basics. We will touch on some topics here in this chapter that we will expand on later in the book but understanding that you need to start at the beginning and not dive into more advanced topics or getting your feet wet in the beginning will lead to failure.

When reading books like these, many people will get a little bit of information and then go and try it. However, they will gloss over this information, come to a conclusion or worse, invest money and time into the wrong thing. Before jumping in and starting, make sure that you read this book from cover to cover. Then, sit on the information, and read it again.

You will also want to take notes, write down questions and even do extra research on areas that you are interested in.

Beginner's Guide to Being a Real Estate Agent

The real estate industry is a big realm consisting of different professionals, from property managers to builders, government agencies, banks, publishers, and of course, sellers, buyers, and renters.

But it is safe to say that the intermediaries are the key players in the industry. People constantly move between and communicate with these professionals, who are none other than **real estate agents and brokers**.

Real estate agents are the workforce of the entire real estate industry. They work as salesmen, buyers' advocates, analysts, auctioneers, consultants, negotiators, and marketers. Now and then, they also work as appraisers, clerks, and loan officers. These experts cater to their clients even on weekends and nights. Most of the time, they also work well beyond the usual 40 hours a week!

A real estate agent can basically do a bit of everything and anything. In exchange, they receive their **real estate commission** as a form of payment after closing the deal. For this reason, it is not really surprising that the demand for professional real estate agents is on the rise despite a slow market. As a result, more and more people are curious to know if they can also be real estate agents themselves.

Sadly, the moment you finally step into this world, things may seem daunting and scary. When you are a new real estate agent, you will also enter a new world. Aside from not receiving a salary, the real estate school you attended probably **didn't teach you anything** that can guarantee surefire success in the industry.

Why Become a Real Estate Agent?

When you choose to embark on your journey as a real estate agent, you will face a great variety of deals. And with all the different properties and different clients out there, you can expect that you won't have to do the same thing and follow the same routine day in and day out.

But one thing is for sure. The moment you get your hands on your real estate license and begin your professional job as an agent, you can look forward to reaching a significant milestone in your life. Being a real estate agent offers a long list of benefits not only for your professional life but also for your personal life.

The following are some of the most common reasons why you might want to consider becoming a real estate agent:

- Business growth
- Career mobility
- Client referrals
- Flexible schedule
- Helping your clients
- Unlimited income potential

Now that you know the special perks that this profession can offer, it can make it easier for you to decide if you will achieve a sense of satisfaction in this particular career path.

Specific Requirements for Real Estate Agents

As far as requirements are concerned, it is important to remember that these may differ depending on the state where you plan to work.

The most common differences among states in terms of **licensing requirements** for real estate agents include the following:

- **Background Checks**

Most states often conduct background checks on aspiring realtors. However, the standards may differ. For example, many states such as Colorado and Texas may even ask for your fingerprints.

- **Training Requirements**

Several states such as New York and Georgia require 75 hours of real estate education while California may mandate up to 135 hours.

- **Better Accessibility for Lawyers**

This one applies to lawyers who want to practice as real estate agents. In certain states such as Florida, practicing lawyers are exempt from taking certain courses.

- **Educational Rules**

Several states don't require a degree just so you can get your license as a real estate agent. States such as New Jersey and Ohio, on the other hand, require you to have a high school diploma or the equivalent of it.

Aside from these, there are also the standard necessities, and these include the eligibility requirements, pre-licensing education, and real estate licensing exam.

Eligibility Requirements for Real Estate Agents

Once again, it is important to remember that there is no such thing as a **national standard checklist for real estate licensing**. All the different states have their own unique set of rules and requirements, which means that may encounter a few restrictions.

Lots of paperwork might be required or you might also need to complete several training programs, present proofs of employment, go through background checks, and so much more. Additional eligibility requirements that are often different from one state to another may include:

- Education requirements
- Errors and omissions insurance
- Employment proof with a sponsor or managing broker/brokerage
- Minimum hours of coursework
- Rates of passing the exam
- On-the-job training requirements

Pre-licensing Education for Real Estate Agents

Every state requires its real estate agents to have some form of real estate pre-licensing education. After the completion of the coursework, you can only continue further after passing the exam administered by your specific state.

When searching for a real estate school you can attend, make sure you look for accredited schools in your state. A copy of your **certificate of completion is necessary** for finalizing your application for a real estate license.

It is also important to ensure that your chosen school offers classes that are suitable for your specific learning style, whether it is an in-classroom or online experience.

Several courses may also bring various facets together to provide a complete education. Again, these courses may also differ depending on the license you are applying for and the state where you are applying for one. Among the most common relevant courses may include:

- Business law
- Law of contracts
- Property management
- Real estate brokerage
- Real estate finance
- Real estate fundamentals
- Real estate law
- Real estate principles

There are lots of options available that you can fit into your schedule. Just don't forget to get your certificates and transcripts afterward which will confirm that you have completed your coursework.

The Real Estate Licensing Exam

A third party is in charge of administering your licensing exam most of the time. It is important to confirm that the specific testing center you choose has been approved for administering the test. You have to **pass both the national and state sections of the exam**. Several states might take these together for you to get your real estate license.

Obtaining Your Real Estate License

Obtaining your real estate license is the first and most critical tip for a real estate agent for beginners. After all, you won't be able to work as a real estate agent without a license so it is a must to take the necessary courses.

While it has already been mentioned above, it is important to reiterate once again the steps you need to take and follow so you can start working to getting your real estate license:

1. Research the specific requirements in your state.

There is no national real estate license, and it means you will have to research the requirements of your state. The requirements of every state may differ according to continuing education, background checks, fees, exams, education, age, and more.

2. Finish your pre-licensing course.

It doesn't matter which state you are looking to get your license in. You will need to take and complete a pre-licensing school that you can do through a local real estate licensing school.

3. Pass the real estate licensing exam.

The pre-licensing course you took serves as your stepping stone and preparation for the final exam which is basically a test that covers laws, practices, and regulations applicable to the state you are applying in.

4. Activate your real estate license.

After successfully passing your real estate exam, all there is left for you to do is activate your real estate license to officially become a real estate agent.

The good news is that you don't need to do everything alone as far as obtaining your real estate license is concerned. You can consider

enrolling in a real estate coaching program *that can help you polish and improve your skills and expand your business.*

Now that you have your core understanding of what is required to legally get into the real estate game, we will expand off into different areas that you will need to focus on. These areas will ensure that you are setup for success and won't make common mistakes that could cost you that million-dollar deal.

8 Daily Routine and Schedule of a Successful Real Estate Agent

Are you aware of the importance of daily routines to make a successful real estate agent? Well, you should! A successful real estate agent uses an organized and scheduled timetable to ensure their businesses stay on track. These routines are also used by highly successful people in any industry. If you simply roll with the punches or fly by the seat of your pants, you will constantly be looking for new opportunities and wondering why you are not moving forward.

However, when creating a routine that fits you and your lifestyle, you can control the actions that occur around you and adjust and pivot when things are either going well or not so well. To be blindsided by a dip in the market or even someone trying to home in on one of your prospects can make you do a double take. However, if you are focused on your routine, these can easily be avoided and dealt with.

1. Productive morning ritual

Top of the morning to you! This should be the first part of your day, from getting out of bed to getting dressed and ready to go. Let's say, from 5 am to 8 am.

A regular, delightful morning ritual will get your day off to a good start. The **world's most successful people are usually early risers** and have some form of morning ritual.

Use this opportunity to refuel your body and energize yourself for the hectic day ahead! Spending time preparing for your day will ensure that you are fully ready for whatever plans you have.

The agent lifestyle might be hectic but starting the day mindfully will help you stay bright and ready for the tasks ahead.

Set yourself up for success by putting yourself in a high mental condition. We propose prayer, meditation, visualization, audiobooks, gratitude, journaling, and affirmations if you don't already have a morning routine.

You must also remember your personal responsibilities. This could include tasks like taking out the garbage, walking the dog, driving your children to school, and cleaning up around the house.

It could even be jogging, walking, or riding your bike.

Just make sure to **start your day with a focused ritual**. Whatever it is, you need a routine to keep you grounded and start your day off with a positive mindset.

After this ritual, you can begin brushing, bathing, and getting dressed.

2. Quick Daily Overview

Connect with your assistant or look at your day planner and go over your aims and outcomes for the day. Make and carry out your social media marketing strategy.

Spend some time checking your email and responding where necessary. Check to see if you have everything you could possibly need to be productive for the day.

To get a handle on the local market, start with the Hot Sheet. By **using platforms like BoomTown**, you can see new listings, status changes, price updates, and more.

Begin cold calling, networking, and contacting previous clients. To generate new business, you'll need to spend some time daily phoning prospects, referrals, and existing clients, and it's best to do it before rush hour.

Also, **practice scripts and role-playing** instead of jumping in and talking to real people on the phone straight away. Role-playing can help you improve your negotiation skills, conversion scripts, and objection handlers.

These should be done between 8 am and 9 am as you sip your coffee or have breakfast. To save time, some of this can be done in the car as you drive to work; just make sure to get it done.

3. Block your schedule

Your day has started now; you're in your office or at your firm, wherever your base of operation is.

It's time to **put your schedule in blocks**. No distractions; just take time for setting appointments in order. Preferably from 9 am to 10:30 am. It's tempting to jump from one task to the next but doing similar things in the same block of time is far more efficient.

Schedule specified time intervals for generating leads, following up on leads, responding to emails, showing appointments, and other meetings.

You won't have to worry about fitting in more minor work between meetings this way. Because homes and properties come and go on the market every minute, you'll need to alter your calendar quickly to accommodate everyone.

The same can be said for marketing efforts. It can be challenging to get back on track when you switch from building a marketing plan to fielding phone calls. As a result, focusing on one type of task at a time is a better use of your time.

Setting aside time for each task ensures that you will complete the important tasks even if other distractions arise. Make a preference scale and stick to it to help **block your schedule in time cells**. Arrange your day's chores in the order of priority to you.

There is a clear distinction between what you want to do and what you need to do. You'll feel more accomplished throughout the day if you first complete the most essential task. It's remarkable how doing one activity may significantly impact the rest of your day.

4. Get to work

This is the main part of your day. It could be from 10:30 am to 4:30 pm. The significant parts of a successful real estate agents work can be broken down into:

Administrative Work

For specialized agents, i.e., solely a seller's agent or a buyer's agent, your administrative work will be specific.

For Seller's agents:

Your job is to prepare a comparative marketing analysis report to research listings at various stages, determine a listing price for properties, prepare a listing presentation, coordinate with stagers, list properties for sale, host open houses, and represent the Seller during a buyer's walk-through inspection.

For a Buyer's agent:

Searching the MLS for new and appropriate listings, touring new listings at least once a week or once a month to find suitable properties for the buyers, showing properties, walking through inspections, providing the buyer with important contacts, meeting with other agents in your brokerage to discuss listings, and meeting with loan officers to expand your network and establish a referral source.

Regardless of your specialty, a big chunk of your administrative are:

Creating promotional marketing materials for you or your properties, networking with potential clients and referral sources, brushing up on any new real estate regulations, setting up and adhering to a monthly budget, managing and posting on social media, and responding to emails, texts, and phone calls.

Generating And Following Up on Leads

Real estate brokers do not generate money unless they have clients; thus, maintaining a list of leads should be prioritized. Whether this list of potential new clients is the product of your marketing efforts, word of mouth, or returning customers, you must constantly be aware of where your next sale could be coming from.

If marketing activities generate most of your leads, you will need to market your services daily.

Following up on leads is critical after they are generated. Make time to contact the prospects you've identified as potential clients. This demonstrates your commitment to finding them the finest discounts available.

Playing The Middleman

You will frequently act as a go-between for your clients, mortgage providers, and other real estate agents. You must be skilled in problem resolution and negotiation.

You must play the **emotionally neutral participant** to keep your client's emotions in check. There is no way out of this role, no matter where you are in your career. It's simply part of the job.

5. Take a Break

In between your working hours, **take out time to rest a little**. Take a brisk walk to mentally refuel before beginning your next task.

Take a moment to contact someone in your family, go through social media, have lunch, or simply relax.

Now we've handled the significant parts of the day!

6. Daily Wrap-Up

Close the day by reflecting on what you did and **setting goals for tomorrow**.

On days where you achieved as much as you planned to, give yourself a pat on the back. On days when it is the opposite, be honest with yourself and strive to do better the next day.

This should be between 4:30 pm and 5 pm.

7. Relationship building

You've left the office to go home to your family or out for drinks with some friends. Remember that you can still work during this time. A successful agent's job revolves around how many people he can relate to.

Call past clients in the car on your way home from work to check in; nothing official. If you happen to pass by their houses, you could even say hello.

If you're out with friends, **don't be afraid to approach new people**, tell them about your work, hand out your business card, and engage them in conversation. It's best to do this after people have been uptight during their regular working hours. You never know who has a house to sell or is planning to buy one.

You should be finished by 7:00 pm and on your way home.

8. Self Revitalization

Get home, take a shower and renew the day's lost energy.

It can be by relating with the kids and the spouse, or just watching TV, playing video games, listening to the news, or even taking a deep bath. For some, it is as simple as eating a good meal.

Regardless of how you recharge, ensure you do this to **get your body in shape for another day's work**. By 9:00 pm, you should be done with this and getting ready to go to bed.

Have a good night's rest and be up by 5 am for another productive day as a successful real estate agent!

The 6 Mindsets of Highly Successful Real Estate Agents

Now that you have created your routine and are starting to become accustomed to it, the next step is to work on your mindset. At this point you should be feeling pretty good. You have passed your tests, acquired your license and are looking forward to a profitable career.

If this is you, the next thing you need to do is take a step back and look at what your next actions will be. If you don't and simply jump ahead and try to move forward, you will quickly find yourself in a situation you don't know how to get out of. It is important that you get out of your own way of your success. Simply because you have a license and can sell real estate, doesn't mean someone more experienced won't come in and knock you down to before you started.

This is why developing your core mindset is key. With a positive mindset combined with your routine, you stand a greater chance for success. So, here are six key components to developing your mindset for real estate and beyond.

1. Ditch the Fixed Mindset for a Growth Mindset

A growth and development mindset will allow you to be resilient for any shortcomings in your career. This mindset helps your brain understand that you'll encounter some setbacks and challenges in your journey.

On the other hand, a fixed mindset makes you think that you must be perfect. If you fail at something and you have a fixed mindset, **you label yourself as a failure**.

With a fixed mindset, you're focused on the final outcome instead of the journey. You give up if you encounter a stumbling block since your mind doesn't understand that you can develop special skills along the way and learn from your mistakes.

In addition, realtors with a fixed mindset are threatened by the success of other agents. They think successful agents are born with a silver spoon in their mouths and can only envy them.

However, a growth mindset will inspire you when other agents succeed at what they do. You'll ask them questions and ask for feedback, then **use positive criticism to motivate you**. Besides, you'll ask your successful peers to become your mentors and give you advice along your journey.

Real estate agents with fixed mindsets often delay their growth since they view themselves as people without talent. They think it's impossible to excel.

Focus on the positive side of things, take on more challenges, and be patient with your growth. This is a growth mindset.

2. Fail Forward

Many new real estate agents are afraid of failure. They think that failure is the end of their career. On the other hand, successful realtors embrace failure and understand that it's the fuel for their growth.

Keep in mind that real estate is often a trial-and-error process. You don't have to settle for one strategy even when it's not working. If you fail at one thing, it shouldn't stop you from trying something else. Don't lose your passion for something you love.

Successful realtors **let their failures motivate them** to do better in their careers. Always look at things objectively. Determine what went wrong and what you need to change. You can then use that to improve your skills.

Ensure you regularly check yourself to avoid going off track. This prevents you from falling back into the same failures that you're trying to avoid. These real estate affirmations can motivate you to achieve all your goals and overcome your fear and stress.

3. Networking is Crucial to Success

Real estate is a networking game. As the old adage goes, if you want to go fast, walk alone, but if you want to go far, walk with others. Besides, you're only as good as the people you surround yourself with.

Sometimes, what looks like a one-man show actually takes a whole lot of people to achieve. You can achieve a lot of growth in your career by walking with mentors, career coaches, business partners, and any other connections.

At the start of your real estate career, you need to be **more intentional about networking**. Attend industry events such as seminars, workshops, and conferences. These are great avenues to meet other real estate agents who could become partners or mentors. Ask them what skills or tips you need to succeed in your career. Don't forget to ask them to give you some of their listings.

Don't only network with industry professionals. Any single interaction with a potential client is a chance to add someone to your network. You don't always have to make a sale. Make a good impression so they can always remember you and refer you to someone else in need of your services.

At the end of the day, keep in mind that the **quality of people in your network** is far more important than the quantity. Successful realtors understand that knowing the right people may help them achieve more than they could possibly do alone.

4. Integrity Over Money

Successful real estate agents are confident because they're honest and have integrity. They mean what they say and must deliver on what they promise their clients. They understand that you can't build a successful career without honesty and integrity.

Put yourself in your client's shoes. Would you hire an agent you can't trust? Would you work with an agent who doesn't keep their word? Do you want a realtor who puts money before everything else and fails to offer value? Would you work with an agent who has no values or principles?

Your **honesty and integrity** will be key in setting a good foundation for your career. Agents who are integrity-driven always ensure that they're making the best decision in their careers. Always do the right thing even when it means losing a sale. Your client will appreciate it when you have their best interest at heart. Love what you do and do it right.

5. Discipline Trumps Motivation

While you may be passionate about your real estate career, the truth is that you won't be motivated every day to keep working. There are some days when the alarm clock will sound like a bother and you won't feel like leaving your bed. There will be other days when the weather will be too harsh for you to attend meetings and appointments.

Don't worry if this happens to you. Many successful real estate agents have these phases as well. What makes the difference is that they realize motivation is transient. It wears out sooner than you realize it.

As such, never wait for motivation to get into action. **What you need is discipline**. Discipline will have you doing what you set out to do even when you don't feel like it. It also flips your mindset from having to do something to wanting to do it.

Have systems in place to ensure that you achieve your tasks even when your motivation is low. Systems will work for you in the long term. They also ensure that your business is still running even when you're not present. You can be on vacation and your marketing is still going on as usual.

Examples of systems that you can implement include customer relationship management (CRM) systems, business management systems, and lead generation software. Determine what systems you need to use and implement them to ensure you won't have to micromanage every single aspect of your business.

6. The Abundance Mindset

Always see the glass as half-full, not half-empty. This is a simple way to have an abundance mindset. Change your perspective.

Successful real estate agents remain **optimistic and hopeful for success**. This is the mindset that will help you make steps into the unknown, embrace your fears, and use failure as fuel for growth. The abundance mindset teaches you that there's a lot of knowledge, tools, and resources to take advantage of in your journey.

With an abundance mindset, you won't be dejected if a promising deal falls through. Instead, you'll see the client as a new asset in your network. They will come back one day and become a long-term client. The client will also introduce you to other people in their networks and keep your client pipeline full.

An abundance mindset lets you see other real estate agents **as partners and collaborators** instead of rivals. Understand that you could learn many things from them about what to do and what not to do. Besides, you could partner with them on many big deals.

An abundance mindset is filled with gratitude. Realize that the real estate world is filled with immense opportunities for you to maximize. Helping others reach their goals helps you achieve yours as well.

Your First 30 Days as a New Real Estate Agent

We understand that the first few months as a real estate agent can be overwhelming. Thankfully, things get easier with time. If you've come to a crossroads and you don't know what direction to take, know that yours isn't an isolated experience. Every real estate agent has gone through what you're going through.

As a new realtor, know that clients will not work with you because you're new. Many will decline working with you due to your lack of confidence. You need to look and act like you know what you're doing and why you're doing it.

There's a lot of advice out there for new real estate agents. However, not all advice is given in a relatable way. This is why we'll be looking at what you should focus on during your first 30 days as a new real estate agent. Some of these tips are insider secrets from seasoned realtors, so be sure to go through everything.

Build Your Network

As we always say, relationships are a vital aspect of real estate. Did you know that 75% of a realtor's business comes from word of mouth and referrals? It's extremely important to build your network and keep expanding it. The more people you know, the greater your chances of getting business.

The first step should be to talk to your **sphere of influence**. Many new agents think that they don't have a sphere of influence, yet they don't know how to identify it. Your sphere of influence includes your immediate family, friends, colleagues, and acquaintances. Start checking with them and reestablish any lost connections. These people are really important since they already know you.

You can now start building your networks in professional circles. Get to know people within your industry. Attend industry events, such as local workshops and seminars. Keep in mind that your **first 30 days**

are for spreading the word. You don't have to necessarily make a sale. Introduce yourself, offer value, and serve others.

Find a Mentor

When building a network, you ought to find a more successful and seasoned real estate agent who's willing to give you advice. If you don't know any top-producing agents, ask other real estate agents in your network for referrals.

Many agents get into the career thinking it's as glamorous as real estate TV shows make it seem. The work of your mentor will be to debunk these common misconceptions. Your real estate mentor will teach you things you can never learn in any school. That's why you must get as much information from them as possible.

Here are a few questions you can ask your mentor:

- What common challenges should I be prepared for?
- What common pitfalls make agents quit?
- How do you source for clients?
- How do you convert leads into clients?
- How do you manage your time?
- What do you struggle with most?
- What books/videos/TV shows should I consume to deepen my knowledge?

Some top-performing real estate agents will gladly let you drink from their fountain of wisdom. Some may look like they want to demonstrate how good they are, but you can **take it as a motivation to become as good as them** (Mindset, remember?).

Don't be afraid to ask them for coffee or lunch. They'll tell you that there are no secrets in real estate. Just like you can't get a beach body in a week, you must work hard and stay resilient. Successful real estate agents achieve great heights because they work hard.

Take this as your first opportunity to start building important relationships. If you can't convince a successful real estate agent to meet you over a cup of coffee, how are you going to convince a client to hire you?

Keep in mind that you must bring something to the table. Offer something to **make your mentor** more than happy to meet you. For example, you can send them a handwritten note to say thank you for meeting you or buy them a gift based on what they like.

Build an Online Presence

While you'll be spending most of your time in your first 30 days building a network and learning the process, don't forget to kick off your marketing strategy. One of the best ways to do this today is by building an online presence.

Google your name and see what comes up. You're likely to see that you need to work on your professional online presence. You might have a few social media accounts but these aren't associated with what you do.

The most popular way to have an online presence is to have a professional website. However, this option may not always favor new agents. You can start by having an online profile on real estate websites, such as Trulia and Zillow.

After that, you can now focus on social media platforms. Open accounts on Facebook, Twitter, Instagram, and LinkedIn. Your goal should be to increase your online visibility. As such, just being present isn't enough.

Post regularly and start thought-provoking conversations. Engage your audience in the comment section and ensure you offer value. Use relevant hashtags on platforms such as Twitter and Instagram to increase your posts' reach.

Lead Generation

When it comes to lead generation for new real estate agents, you need to place yourself where your target clients are. Identify where clients who are ready to buy are and go to them.

Since you may not have a considerable budget yet, you need to choose lead-generation strategies that require sweat equity. Sweat equity strategies require more of your time and effort than money.

One strategy to get clients who are ready to buy is hosting an open house. An open house is a strategy where a property listed for sale is made available to interested buyers to view. This is a perfect strategy for new agents since people who attend are already interested and ready to buy.

So, how much lead generation is enough for a new agent?

The answer is a lot. You must spend a lot of your efforts trying various lead-generation strategies to fill your client pipeline. Remember, you're trying to get clients and determine what works for you at the same time.

The reality is that many newbies underestimate the amount of work required to get their first client. You probably need to make more than 50 cold calls and host more than 20 open houses to get your first client.

This is a lot of effort. There are some agents who might get a client from one open house, but they mostly host a mega open house. The amount of effort that goes into hosting a mega open house is probably the same amount of effort you'll need to host 20.

Keep in mind that you'll have to sacrifice most of your time during your first 30 days as a real estate agent.

Now that you have the basics of what is entailed in being a real estate agent, do you want to continue? If the answer is YES, then we will dive deeper into what you need to know and steps you need to take. Good luck on your journey and I will see you in the next chapter.

8 Powerful Real Estate Lead Generation Ideas for New Agents and Realtors

Generating leads can be difficult for those who are just getting started as real estate agents. In real estate, no lead, no client and so no money! So, it is important to learn how to generate leads as a newbie real estate agent or realtor. Here are the 8 powerful real estate lead generation ideas for new agents and realtors.

Use Google

Google is more than simply a search engine for you as a new real estate agent. It is true that Google dominates the online search business, with 63.5% of all searches passing via its engine.

*That's not all, though! Ever heard of **Google My Business**?*

Google My Business is a free platform offered by Google. It enables business owners to create a unique page to market their brand using photographs, a Google Maps location, and client testimonials.

To be prepared for any new Google algorithms that are announced, you should keep this platform updated and optimized. For company pages that receive enough favorable ratings, it also has a preferential ranking method.

Reviews can have up to 10% of an impact on how search engines rank their search results, among other factors. Create a place for reviews on your email after building your business page. This is a useful method for social proofing and recommendations.

Google Ads is yet another way to use Google!

You can use Google advertisements to promote your real estate company on the search network, display network, Google Shopping network, video campaigns, and app campaigns. One of the Google ad types for real estate is the **Google Lead form extensions**, a marketing tool intended to draw viewers in with a call to action that is placed in a responsive form beneath the ad.

After being built in Google Ads, the lead form extension is then included in a campaign for search, video, and discovery. You may alter the Google lead form extensions to match your real estate marketing objectives, and Google ads are an effective option for lead generation.

Professional website

Your brokerage will most likely provide you with a page on their website as a new agent, but it is critical that you build your own web presence. Every real estate investor who wants to grow their business should **have a brand website**.

From Zillow to Trulia to Realtor.com, each site receives over 80 million unique monthly visitors. This is the type of traffic you need to turn into leads. Your website should include your current listings, contact information, and a section for client testimonials and reviews.

This helps you **develop a personal brand and highlight your strengths**. It also ensures that your presence in the local market remains consistent, even if you change brokerages.

In addition, the website should function as a direct lead generation tool. The simplest method is to include lead generation forms on your website. Lead generation forms are online forms that website visitors can use to provide their contact information.

Don't forget to optimize your website. Search Engine Optimization is one of the most effective marketing techniques available to investors.

It is the practice of optimizing your web content so that a search engine will show it as the first result for a specific keyword search. So, when someone searches keywords or terms like "realtor," "real estate agent," "best real estate agents," etc., you want your website to appear on the first page.

Community Marketing

Charity, as the saying goes, begins at home. So, what better place to begin than in your own backyard? **Participate in your community**.

Make an effort to meet with local companies, contractors, and repairmen. Participate in all of the town's major events, and consider setting up a booth if it will aid in networking.

The idea is to create a referral network of people who can help generate new leads. Discover what the residents enjoy and keep it on hand, or discuss it during open house events.

The neighborhood where you work and reside might be a great source of leads. You can become a trusted source of real estate information by building your brand and reputation in the community.

Word of mouth and personal validation are powerful tools that work without your intervention—the simplest form of lead generation.

As a result, maintain a positive relationship with your neighbors. Make those in your neighborhood your first call when they want to purchase or sell a house.

Community pages

Buyers and sellers can find property information on your real estate website's community page.

Community pages are a significant source of content for your website. It provides up-to-date information to buyers and sellers, such as the population of the neighborhood where you work and reside, the cost of living there, history, demographics, and other helpful information.

People looking for properties in a specific location can find your website through search engines, click through, and conduct research on houses you have listed on your website in that area. You gain **more**

traffic that can be converted into leads. To convert traffic into leads, give a free pdf of the region in return for visitors' emails, for example. This will allow you to stay in touch with them and nurture them into clients.

There are additional sections where you may address frequently asked questions about the region. Answering these questions clearly and systematically can boost the website's authority in prospects' minds and increase its Google rating.

When done correctly, you should appear on the top page of Google when someone searches for 'Realtor city-state' or 'real estate agent city-state.' Prospects conducting searches like this want to hire a real estate agent immediately.

Social Media

You represent your brand as a real estate agent. And if you want to survive in today's market, you need a **strong social media presence**, just like any other brand.

In recent years, social media platforms have given real estate agents a platform to market homes, network with other agents, and cultivate relationships with potential clients.

Make sure you have profiles on platforms, such as Facebook, Twitter, and Instagram. You can promote yourself and your listings using any of these platforms. They provide potential customers with a tangible point of reference so they can learn more about you and your offerings.

Also utilize online communities such as Facebook groups, Twitter conversations, and Instagram comment areas to attract leads and promote yourself as a competent, helpful, and consulting resource for potential clients.

We also have some powerful tools to help your social media marketing. Check the description below or go to soldouthouses.com for more details!

LinkedIn Leads

Many still overlook LinkedIn, a service intended just for professional contacts. Whether you like it or not, LinkedIn has overtaken other social media as the leader in social business. Instead of competing with celebrity content and news on other social media sites, why not use the site that was built for professional networking?

LinkedIn provides access to a vast professional network, making it ideal for launching **successful real estate lead-generating campaigns**. Post-attention-grabbing content biweekly or weekly to add relevant information. Using this strategy, you will begin to receive connection requests and followers.

Join LinkedIn communities that your target audience is likely to frequent. That might resemble a group for nearby property speculators or one for first-time homebuyers.

Once you've established a connection, give a persuasive pitch, follow up with potential customers, and offer to take their calls to answer any more questions they may have.

When used in conjunction with **LinkedIn's distinctive algorithm**, which meets the needs of potential customers by connecting your company's content with interested parties, your relationship-building strategies will rise to a higher level.

Retargeting advertising on LinkedIn can also be easily set up using platforms like HubSpot, especially when using the contact targeting feature.

Video Marketing

Videos tell the story better than pictures. Listings that include video walk-throughs generate more interest.

According to 68% of marketers, promotional video generates the highest ROI, and 72% of customers say they'd like to learn about a product or service through videos.

Making an educational video about your real estate business will allow you to significantly improve your lead-generating efforts. It saves time for those who are searching for a realtor because their inquiries are answered in the films.

Make a video and share it online! Remember that 86% of home buyers and sellers begin their search online.

Despite the fact that videos are currently the rage, real estate investors haven't fully embraced this marketing trend. A virtual tour of the property can significantly improve the sale of the property.

A video walk-through can be a unique way to generate real estate leads because it can assist potential buyers in visualizing themselves as the property's owners. They can use it to view every room and examine even the most minute features of the house.

A drone can be used to record a video walk-through with a trained pilot operating it. To make the prospects understand that you are the right agent for them, you can run, walk, or fly across the property with them.

Social Media Ads

Another way of using social media for lead generation is using ads. It could be Facebook ads, Twitter, or even Instagram ads.

You can target the right audience with Facebook ads by location, demographics, and interests.

Facebook Leads Ads assists you in **generating real estate leads** at a lower cost on both mobile and desktop. When users click on the Lead advertising, they are taken to a pre-populated form that contains personal information, such as their name and email address. Then, all users have to do is confirm their information or add some information to it before submitting it.

The pre-filled form, which allows for native ad submission, is another feature of Leads Ads. This implies that your potential lead will not have to leave the app to complete your form.

Twitter advertising, like Facebook advertising, can potentially drive significant traffic to your brand. Like other forms of advertising, it requires an awareness of your target audience and their behavior. Twitter ads are very inexpensive to create, and statistics show that users spend 26% more time viewing ads on Twitter than on other platforms.

So all you need is a sufficient marketing budget to run tests over time until you achieve a profitable campaign.

If you want to reach a younger audience for lead generation, you should also think about Instagram and Tiktok ads. Although they are more expensive, they have a larger audience among millennials.

How New Real Estate Agents Get Clients Fast

Are you wondering how you, as a new agent, can get real estate clients fast?

Clients are the life force for any real estate business. They keep the money flowing in and help the business stay afloat. Your success in your realtor career is hinged on your ability to generate leads, convert them into clients, and get them to sign a contract.

Your first client as a new agent may be the most important client in your career. The first client kindles the fire and boosts your confidence.

However, most new real estate agents find themselves struggling to get clients. They realize that they don't know how or where to start. Luckily, it's possible to build a pipeline of great clients even if you're just starting out. In this article, we're going to look at a few methods to build your client roster and kickstart a successful real estate career.

Leverage Your Sphere of Influence

Most successful real estate agents are familiar with the "sphere of influence" since **it's an essential strategy** to kickstart your career. So, what does the sphere of influence mean and how can you use it to get clients fast?

Your sphere of influence refers to the immediate network of people you already know when starting your real estate career. Many new agents make the mistake of thinking that they have no sphere of influence. We all have a sphere of influence, it's just that many people don't know how to identify it.

Your sphere of influence includes your family, friends, acquaintances, colleagues, and basically anyone who knows you. You can work with these people when starting your career and seek professional help, opinions, and even mentorship.

The best thing about this strategy is that the people in your **sphere of influence are already warm leads** should they decide to buy or sell properties. There's a high chance of them hiring you since they already know you.

How do you get started with this strategy?

Simply reach out to your family, friends, and acquaintances, and let them know the kind of services you're offering. Even if they won't become clients themselves, they're likely to recommend you to someone else in their circle who needs to buy or sell.

Expand Your Network

While your sphere of influence can help you get your first few clients, you need a larger circle to build a sustainable leads roster. You need to **expand your circle through networking**. Networking has been proven to be an effective method to generate leads.

In case you don't know how to start networking as a beginner, you can start by attending industry events, such as workshops, seminars or conferences. These events will help you meet other real estate agents who can mentor you or collaborate with you. You'll be surprised by the number of agents willing to tell you about their listings.

Don't only think of networking in professional settings. You could network while doing everyday activities, such as at the gym, book club meetings, talking to a random person at a restaurant, or in discussions in Facebook groups.

Volunteering in your local community is another way to network that's barely spoken about. It's an effective and organic way to network since you get to meet people while giving back. These people may end up trusting you in one of their biggest investment and financial decisions.

The key to networking is to introduce yourself to people and tell them what you do. Prepare a 60-second pitch that highlights who you are, your services, and why you're different from other agents. Let them know your skills and why you'll be valuable to them.

Practice your speech at home so that you don't babble when they ask "what do you do?"

Door-Knocking

Door knocking is arguably the oldest real estate client generation strategy. Many real estate agents have been told to start by door-knocking.

As the name suggests, this strategy involves knocking on doors and talking to the property owners to see if they might be interested in buying or selling a property.

Most new real estate agents fear this strategy understandably because rejection could be demoralizing. However, the key to a **successful door-knocking strategy is offering value.**

When you're offering value, the conversation becomes meaningful even if the homeowner isn't interested in your services. Without value, the conversation isn't worthwhile to the property owner.

How do you provide value while door-knocking?

Think of anything that could educate or improve the property owners' lives. For example, some owners don't know their property's current market value. Show them what it's worth or why that neighborhood could attract good offers.

This may not immediately change their mind to list their homes, but **it may motivate them** to do so in the future.

Maximize Your Digital Presence

In this digital age, you can't afford to ignore the power of online presence. A vibrant online presence has helped many new real estate agents bag clients fast.

Creating an online presence for your business means **having a professional website** that explains what you do along with your contact details. You should also have pages on Facebook, Twitter, LinkedIn, and Instagram, as well as professional profiles on real estate platforms, such as Trulia, Zillow, and Realtor.com. If you can create video content, use TikTok and YouTube pages.

However, you need to understand that just having an online presence isn't enough. You need to engage your audience and get their attention.

Create educational and valuable blog posts for your website. This can help you establish yourself as a thought leader or authority in your local market. Regularly post news or opinion articles on your social media pages. Ensure you engage your audience in the comment sections. The key is to always provide value.

The best thing about social media is that you can use it for marketing. If you already have a listing, you can post high-quality images on your pages along with an in-depth description. Be sure to **use relevant hashtags** to boost visibility.

Cold Calling

Cold calling is much like door knocking, only it's done on the phone. It's referred to as "cold" since you're calling people you don't have a rapport with. Your goal is to see whether they may be **willing to buy or sell a home**.

The secret to successful cold calling is in numbers. The more people you call, the more you increase your chances of listing a client. This strategy is popular since it can be effective.

Just like door-knocking, you can boost your chances of getting a client by offering value. Since you're reaching out to leads while still cold, you can make them warm and pique their interest by offering value. Your value is offering them knowledge and giving them information.

Your cold leads may become warm once they know how much money they could make from a certain sale or by buying a property and offering it for rent. In most cases, the lead **may not be looking to sell or buy**. However, you could be lucky and call someone who's already considering buying or selling.

Automate

Real estate agents, both newbies and experienced, have struggled with reaching out to all their leads and staying connected. However, you can automate and use real estate software to generate more leads and get more clients.

It's tempting to organize all your tasks by yourself since the real estate career requires you to have an independent contractor mindset. Since you want to save money and time, and also make your business easier to manage, **you need to invest in software**.

Customer relationship management (CRM) software will help you keep in touch with your leads. Since your budget as a beginner may not be huge, you can start with free real estate CRMs that can help you in lead generation. For example, these CRM tools can help you automate your email campaigns by consistently reaching out to your leads with custom messages and encouraging business.

CHAPTER TWO

TOOLS AND PREPARING FOR SUCCESS

Now that you have hit the ground running, we are going to move forward in this chapter and assume that you are sitting at your desk with your license ready to dive in and start getting clients. If not, stop, go back to the first chapter and start from the beginning. If you want to have success you need to start at the beginning.

The first thing that we are going to talk about are the tools you can use to get started. When starting any business or entering into any situation, if you don't have the right tools and resources at your disposal, it will be very difficult to move forward. Take your time and gather the correct tools that work best for you. Not everyone will use the same types of tools, so don't be afraid to explore other options and opportunities.

1. Social media marketing tools

Effective social media marketing has the potential to significantly impact the success of your brand. Social media platforms are great for sharing business testimonial stories, a brand's goals and values, interacting emotionally with customers, and enhancing sales.

Social media is extremely significant to 89% of marketers and vital to 30% in terms of their overall marketing strategy.

Using **social media tools** makes it simple to share the same information to numerous profiles and networks with a single click, scheduling and tracking each social message you've made across all of your individual social media profiles and networks.

One of the first and best-known social marketing tools on the market is Hootsuite. It gives you the option to bulk upload up to 350 posts, target posts, add a location, manage privacy, and customize each social network profile.

Thanks to the numerous social media profiles like Facebook, LinkedIn, Instagram, Twitter, and others that are linked to Hootsuite, you can pin your favorite accounts for targeted monitoring. With this feature, you can also review draft posts and schedule posts for the future.

What distinguishes Hootsuite communicates directly with your audience across a variety of channels using a feature-rich dashboard.

Hootsuite is difficult to operate and has a clumsy UI. It could be difficult for new users to understand all the features and categories because there are so many, and the high price is another significant drawback.

Buffer, another social marketing tool, is a **social media scheduling tool** that enables users to conveniently schedule and share posts on social network profiles. Its advantages over Hootsuite include an easy-to-use layout and user experience, scheduling options, and posting tools.

Users of Buffer can schedule posts to be shared at a later time. It assigns pre-scheduled intervals throughout the day where your material will automatically be posted once you specify how many times per day you want the article to be shared by a social media platform.

Social Champ is a **social media scheduling and management tool** that simultaneously spreads your content on all social media platforms. Social Champ is the best option to market your content if you are a novice because of its easy-to-use user interface. Social Champ has excellent customer service which is one of its strongest features.

With its distinctive, data-driven features, Social Champ surpasses Hootsuite and Buffer. The platform also gives users the ability to develop a more appealing and targeted social media presence.

2. Email marketing tools

Email marketing is an essential element of any marketing strategy. With a return on investment of $42 for every $1 spent, email marketing continues to be a great tool for business owners.

If you want to realize the potential of email marketing fully, you must select the ideal tool for advancing your business. **Email marketing tools** enable you to send and track emails, increase your list, and segment it, making them an effective tool for growing your business and generating revenue.

ActiveCampaign is one of the greatest email marketing tools solutions and has hundreds of pre-built automation that personalizes campaigns for each subscriber. By concentrating on creating a top-notch product that offers several solutions for enterprises from all over the world, ActiveCampaign has established itself as a market leader in marketing automation software.

With machine learning and predictive features, it is the most sophisticated email marketing platform, allowing marketers to operate more effectively and provide a higher return of investment. It contains an **integrated CRM system** to manage your sales, provides live chat, and email campaigns and is far more user-friendly and easier to use than some other systems.

You can go to https://getACfreetrial.com to sign up a 14 days free trial of Activecampaign.

3. Video marketing tools

Videos are crucial in real estate. With the use of real estate video marketing, you may introduce potential customers to your homes for sale. This is a breakthrough, especially for brokers and clients who can afford to view **virtual tours of homes** even when they don't live nearby.

Making real estate videos is easy with Animoto video creator. It offers an extensive selection of Animoto video templates from which to create stunning real estate videos. Animoto is a wise choice if you want to create a top-notch real estate video.

InVideo is an inexpensive, user-friendly solution that enables you to expedite your video production without spending a lot of money or time. It has numerous options to modify typefaces, add music, and brand your videos. It also provides sophisticated editing tools, pre-designed layouts, and a useful content repository of images and videos.

4. Graphic design Marketing tools

While intriguing language, blogs, and social media material can aid in differentiating your business from the competition, visitors are more likely to stay engaged if your site or content has a visually appealing design. Therefore, making graphic designs that are both aesthetically pleasing and contextually relevant is essential.

With Adobe Illustrator, you can make anything from online and mobile graphics to logos, icons, book illustrations, product packaging, billboards, and so much more. Adobe Illustrator makes use of AI to automatically apply colors from photos to your design and auto-trace hand-drawn sketches to create vector graphics.

Another tool for graphic design is Canva. It is used to generate social media graphics, documents, posters, and other visual content. Using Canva, you can select from a wide range of ready-made templates and pick graphic design assets like images, illustrations & icons to best match your brand. It is relatively easy to use and works on all devices, unlike Adobe Photoshop, which works on computers only.

A major shortfall in Canva is that it lacks templates specifically designed for realtors. However, we provide over 1700+ real estate templates at our pro membership that'll solve your every design need. You can check them out at https://soldouthouses.com/pro/

5. Website builder tools

Digitizing your business is a need rather than an option. One cannot undervalue the importance of having an excellent online presence.

In the early days of the Internet, learning to code was a requirement if you wanted to create a website. Thankfully, **website builders are**

now available tools for users to construct stunning websites without having any programming experience.

One of the most widely used website builders for real estate agents to display their listings is WordPress. You can create a website, edit pages, and manage your blog using a single platform. WordPress can, however, be extremely vulnerable and expensive to maintain.

If you want to personalize your WordPress website uniquely or enhance its appearance, you may need to write a lot of complex code lines. You also need to be knowledgeable in HTML, CSS, and PHP to make certain modifications to your WordPress website.

Clickfunnels, another efficient app, is a website and a **sales funnel builder tool for realtors**. This makes it a better option for realtors and goes a step further to help you build your brand, make sales, and generate more leads for your business.

You can go to https://getCFfreetrial.com to sign up a 14 days free trial of Clickfunnnels.

6. Analytic marketing tools

Software programs known as marketing analytics tools are used by firms to monitor their marketing initiatives, better understand their target market, and evaluate the outcomes of their marketing campaigns.

By using the right **marketing analytics software**, advertisers can use their time and resources more wisely, achieve better outcomes, and have a clearer understanding of the effects of each marketing campaign.

One of the strongest SEO tools available is, without a doubt, SEMrush. It provides your keyword research, keeps tabs on your rivals' tactics, performs an SEO audit of your blog, and much more. Semrush has earned the trust of online marketers, which is why corporations like Apple, Amazon, and Samsung use this tool. SEMrush's enormous database boasts over 20 billion keywords and 808 million domains. From strategy to research to optimization and beyond, using SEMrush can significantly impact your content marketing.

Another popular **marketing analytics tool** is Google Analytics. It's a free online analytics service that provides detailed information about visitors to your website or social media pages, such as their hobbies, age, gender, and even location. It helps you understand which social platforms to target, what kind of content you should write, why visitors are leaving your site, and much more. Google Analytics provides valuable insights that can help you to shape your business and spend money only on profitable ventures.

When it comes to tools, don't become overwhelmed. Many people will think they need to invest a lot of money into each and every one of these tools. This is not the case. You want to start small, find what works for you and then expand as your business grows. Also, don't be afraid to try some of these tools out. Many will have a trial period that you can look around and use. Take advantage of these as well.

No matter what tools you use, make sure that you are in control of your data and that you backup everything that you have. The last thing you want to have happen is a company to go out of business or change their business model leaving you with nothing after you have built up your real estate empire. Backup, store in a safe place, rinse, and repeat.

7.All-In-One Digial Marketing Tool

If all of the above seems overwhelming, investing in an all-in-one marketing tool is another excellent alternative.

For example, GoHighLevel is a great all-in-one platform that includes Email marketing software, social media marketing software, funnel building software, analytics software, and even pipeline management software; You can sign up for 14 day free trial at https://getHLfreetrial.com.

You can also join Sold Out Houses Pro membership to get access to all the marketing templates you need to success in real estate; you can get a 14 day free trial at https://soldouthouses.com/pro/

How To Write a Real Estate Agent Business Plan In 10 Steps

Once you have your tools, the next step is to start building a business plan. A business plan is vital to your success. It helps you to determine what you want to do, what you don't want to do, how you want to proceed, what to do when something goes wrong and so much more. When developing your business plan, don't gloss over any of the smaller details. These smaller details could mean success or total failure.

What is a Real Estate Agent Business Plan?

A real estate agent business plan creates guidance and sets the foundation for income goals, goal setting, marketing strategies, understanding of the competitive landscape, and lead generation.

The plan details basic business information including your mission statement and assesses the **strengths, weaknesses, opportunities, and threats** (SWOT) of your organization. Business plans must also include financial calculations and measurable calculations you can revisit during the year to guarantee that you will achieve your goals.

Write Your Mission Statement

Your real estate agent business plan must always begin with your mission statement that identifies your values and the reason for the existence of your business. The mission statement serves as your guide to reaching the ultimate objectives of your business.

When creating an **influential and strong mission statement**, the rest of the items included in your business plan must be targeted at satisfying this statement.

The mission statement must identify your target market or audience, the services or products you offer, and what sets your business apart from the rest. A powerful and effective mission statement must be concise and short but still sums up the objective of the business.

Define Your Why

Your why or your reason why you pursued this career and started this business will serve as your foundation for how you will run your business. It is your vision and without this particular step, **you might right losing your purpose** which will deter and confuse your clients in turn.

Some of the things you need to ponder on include the problem you can solve for clients and your reason for wanting to succeed with your business.

When establishing your brand, during interviews, in times of stress, or even when just engaging in casual conversations, your why keeps you motivated to stand out from the crowd and push forward no matter what.

Perform a SWOT Analysis

The acronym SWOT standards for the strengths, weaknesses, opportunities, and threats of a business or organization. The main objective of the said four elements is to evaluate a business through an assessment of the external and internal factors that can help you make more money and drive your decision-making.

Conducting a SWOT analysis while developing your real estate agent business plan will **help uncover more opportunities** that will set you apart from all your existing competition on the market.

Set Measurable and Specific Goals

After you have clearly defined your mission and vision and performed a SWOT analysis, it is now time for you to set goals for your business. Your goals will help set the tone to improve your performance and steer your business in the right direction. The goals you set must also have a clear way of showing your progress that will serve as the key motivator to ensure that you stay on track to reaching them.

Every goal you make must follow a pattern to determine set criteria. Doing so will guarantee that your everyday efforts are done to meet the objectives of the business within a short timeframe. An easy way to do it is with the **use of SMART goals.**

You also need to split your goals into long-term and short-term ones. The lengths of your short-term goals may vary between several days or weeks without exceeding six months. You also need to work on these short-term goals as you work on their long-term counterparts.

Meanwhile, long-term goals are those that take up six months or more to finish and need perseverance and careful planning to achieve. Having a nice mix of **long-term and short-term goals** can help you stay motivated.

While all goals are equally critical, success stems from the way you prioritize each one. Add a new goal slowly as you feel comfortable with the present progress of your existing set of goals and as you gain the capacity to do so.

Not identifying your business goals is like leaving your results up to luck to achieve your business activities.

Identify Your Niche

If you think that all real estate agents sell houses, you might want to think again. if every agent is doing the same thing, there wouldn't be a large market, fierce competition, or real estate influencers.

Some realtors focus on luxury single-family houses while others are experts in waterfront condos. **What niche would you want to work on?** Here are a few questions to answer when finding your niche:

- Are you a humble real estate agent in the suburbs or a luxury one based in the metro?
- Do you have additional certifications?
- What type of demographic do you wish to serve?

- What type of services do you offer that others don't?
- What kinds of living spaces do you love?

The answer to these questions will help you establish your distinct brand.

Come Up with Marketing Tactics and Strategies

Developing and implementing marketing tactics and strategies will help you locate and identify your current value proposition in the industry together with specific execution timelines.

Aside from identifying the **overall goals and objectives** of your business, you also need to include the following in your marketing plan and strategy:

- Analyze your market competition
- Create a timeline and set your business plan in motion
- Estimate your projected budget for marketing
- Pinpoint your unique selling proposition
- Identify your target audience and learn your geographic farm area data
- Determine your general marketing goals
- Track your progress and adjust as necessary

Although a marketing strategy determines your business's overall marketing goals, coming up with marketing tactics can help you reach these individual goals. These goals can include tactics for referral business, efforts on retention, and methods for new customer acquisition.

For instance, you can provide incentives to those who will refer your business who closes. You can also implement new **email drip campaigns** that can boost your lead conversion rates.

These strategies must also have set KPIs or key performance indicators to help you assess your performance. A KPI you can set for your business, for example, is for referral business to go beyond 20% of your existing lead generation sources.

Create a Lead Generation and Nurturing Strategy

A successful strategy for lead generation will help you sustain business growth. You can do it through paid ads and organically to attract and convert potential clients. Aside from lead generation, agents must have some systems in place for managing, nurturing, and re-engaging with contacts to increase opportunities.

Lead generation using a multipronged approach is an ideal method for maintaining a good lead flow. You can use common organic strategies such as reaching out to your own sphere of influence, attending networking events, and hosting an open house.

You can also use paid generation methods like buying leads from a lead generation agency or setting up a dedicated site for funneling potential clients. Your marketing tactics must be directly correlated to your lead generation tactics.

Each lead is a good opportunity even when they might not convert to a deal immediately. Nurturing leads effectively will ensure that no opportunity is amiss. Real estate agents can nurture these leads by constantly developing and engaging relationships with potential leads. You also have to provide potential clients with a regular flow of relevant and important information which depends on where they are in the process.

It will be easier to nurture leads if you **implement an efficient CRM or customer relationship management tool.** Many CRMs are affordable and can gather all contacts into a single easy-to-use platform.

Real estate agents can input contact details together with other necessary notes into the profile of the contact to refer back to during communication with leads.

Focus on Budgeting

Keeping track of your budgeting and finances is crucial to understand how to continue running your business, especially if you are an independent contractor. Keep a record of dates and categorize them to know where your money goes and where it comes from exactly.

Items you can consider when considering your budget on your real estate agent business plan include the following:

- Should you hire a transaction coordinator?
- How many houses have you sold for the past 6 months?
- How much will you spend on marketing every listing?
- What are your car expenses?
- What is your commission split?
- What is the average sales price in your niche?

Don't forget to include the **expense reviews monthly** to be more familiar with your finance sheets. By doing so, you will know how to use your money and time more efficiently.

Compute Your Income Goal

Your income goal is another important item you should include in your real estate agent business plan. Although it might be harder for new agents who might still be trying to learn the ropes of the business, you still need to estimate how much you will earn for a year.

You can work with a professional mentor or agent to help you estimate your income goals. If you are a seasoned agent, review your past years to **determine your monetary goals** for the next year.

You need a few basic figure estimates to compute your income goal and how much work you need to make to reach that goal, which includes the following:

- **Estimate of accomplished deals yearly**

Estimate how many deals you want to complete in a year. Remember that some months won't be as busy as others, so always consider your personal schedule, holidays, and weather.

- **Fee split with brokerage**

It is the agreed-upon commission split you make with your brokerage for every completed transaction. If you have a 70/30 split with your brokerage, for example, you will receive 70% of the commission while your brokerage will get 30% commission for every deal.

- **Net income**

Net income is the amount of money that will go into your pocket after you split the commission with the brokerage.

You can give yourself a more realistic figure for your income goal if you determine these numbers. Compute for the GCI or gross income commission or the amount of money you should make before the commission splits as well as the average profit per month and per deal you will need to achieve your goal.

Review Your Business Plan Regularly

A business plan won't be effective if you don't use it at all. Your real estate agent business plan serves as the roadmap for your business. As such, you need to revisit and review it as often as you can to ensure that you stay right on track and don't veer on the wrong path.

Your plan should serve as a constant resource that will guide you through achieving your business objectives and goals. However, it doesn't mean it is set in stone, though, especially if you have to make a few changes.

As a real estate agent, you have to **revisit your business plan every month** to help you measure and track your progress and add the necessary changes and tweaks to stay on the right path. Once you discover that you are missing some of the set times for your goals, you have to continue revisiting your business plan regularly.

Making updates to your business plant itself must be done every year after you have developed a complete picture of your yearly performance. Evaluation of your business plan will help you learn new tactics and strategies and make sure that you have the necessary resources for the coming year.

Now that you know **how to write a real estate agent business plan**, you will be more ready to face anything that might come your way as your business grows and expands.

Personal Branding for Real Estate Agents –Rules to Become the Top-Of-Mind of Your Ideal Clients

Now that you have your business plan in place and you have the tools you need to succeed, it is time to take a step back and develop your personal brand. In the real estate game and in other industries, people can buy from anyone. Just because you have a suit and business cards and a fancy website, doesn't mean that you will get the sale over someone else. This is why it is important that you create a personal brand.

This personal brand will show who you are, what you stand for and reflect you as a person. When looking at large companies like Coldwell Banker, Keller Williams, Berkshire Hathaway, and RE/MAX, they have all created established brands and have made their stand in the market. As a real estate agent, you need to either work for these companies, or you need to create and establish your brand.

It is stated that the most important component in creating your brand is your logo. Since most people will connect with a good logo, it should be the first thing that you focus on.

Here are some stats.

- 84% of consumers correctly identified Berkshire Hathaway by its font alone.
- 91% of consumers correctly identified Coldwell Banker by its color scheme.
- 90% of consumers correctly identified RE/MAX's imagery of colors and balloons. However, without that imagery, only 63% could correctly identify its font.

- 81% of consumers correctly identified Keller Williams by its color scheme.
- 30% of consumers could correctly identify Century 21's current logo due to confusion over a recent rebranding.

When it comes to developing your brand, don't spend five minute on it. Spend months.

Determine What Makes You Different

Once you've defined your target customers, it's now time to focus on your abilities and what you can offer. Focus on what makes you different since clients want to work with an agent whose personality and vision match theirs.

You can ask yourself a few questions to identify what makes you stand out:

- Why did I choose a real estate agent career?
- Do I have goals that drive my career?
- Why should the clients choose me instead of another agent?
- If I were a client, would I buy a property from myself?
- In what areas do I specialize?
- What kind of feedback do I get from my clients?
- How do I make the buying process easier for my clients?

Ensure that your questions are specific since this helps you create better messages on what makes you unique. You want your brand messaging to focus on why working with you is a huge benefit. This way you can generate more leads, convert them into clients, and grow your career.

However, keep in mind that honesty is the key. Don't lie to yourself or to the audience. You don't want to breach the trust you're building. Be true to yourself.

Craft a Distinctive Message

Now, it's time to think about what message you want to pass on to your audience. Your message will help you keep your brand at the top of clients' minds.

One of the most essential aspects of creating a distinctive message is sharing your purpose. You want to **communicate your "why" to your clients**. This aspect helps your audience see how you can help meet their needs.

Another unique messaging tip is sharing your story. Remember, your clients want to feel like they have a personal relationship with you. Narrate a compact version of your life story to help your audience resonate with you.

As we mentioned in a previous tip, stay transparent. **Telling a personal, relatable story** is one way to stay honest and communicate who you are. As well, it'll help communicate your credibility since you demonstrate that you stay true to who you say you are.

While you might not realize it, your audience is already analyzing your abilities and skills for a job even while you may not know them yet.

Come Up with an Effective Marketing Strategy

A unique message won't achieve the desired effect until you find a way to spread the word. You need an effective marketing strategy to pass your message to your target audience.

We live in the digital era where a large percentage of the world's population relies on the internet daily for information and other services. Any brand that lacks a digital marketing strategy is missing out on the diverse opportunities it offers.

One of the first steps in creating an effective marketing strategy is having an online presence. An effective online presence goes beyond **having a basic website** with just your name and contact details. Your online presence needs to create a channel for you to access a large pool of leads and allow your clients to reach you at any time of the day.

Next, you want to create content that generates leads and converts them into clients. Your content must answer your target audience's needs. Again, this is where defining your audience comes into play. Ensure your content answers any questions they may have about the buying and selling of real estate or any other processes.

Once you have the content, make sure you're spreading it on the right channels. Here are a few pointers to help you spread the word:

- **Social media**– A majority of internet users never go a day without logging into at least one social media platform. It is important to understand how to leverage social media to grow your business. Once you have a presence on common platforms, such as Facebook, Instagram, Twitter, and LinkedIn, post regularly and engage in impactful conversations with your audience. The key is to ensure that you're providing value to your social media audience.
- **Video content**– Video content is becoming more popular with the advent of platforms, such as YouTube, TikTok, and

Instagram reels. In fact, 86% of marketers online are already using video content. Short but informative videos can be extremely efficient in helping you deliver your message.

- **Blog posts**– Blog posts are important in building credibility and trust since they demonstrate your authority and expertise in the subject matter. They also allow you to pass the message directly without having to include self-promotional material. For example, you can use **blog posts to educate your clients** on how to complete common real estate transactions or how to avoid common newbie pitfalls.

Be Consistent

Brand building is a marathon, not a sprint. You need to have a long-term mindset when building your brand. Look at some of the successful brands, such as Coca-Cola, Apple, Amazon, Microsoft, and many others.

While these brands may change their look and language once in a few years, they never deviate from the main message. If you monitor the changes from the beginning, you will notice the changes are usually small and mainly made to just keep up with trends. Besides, **staying consistent helps you stay memorable to your clients**.

Smart brands take time during their branding years to set a strong foundation for their branding efforts. Staying consistent with your brand also generates more brand awareness and develops a sound reputation. Give your brand time and stay consistent.

For example, if you have a sleek logo on your social media pages, but you have a playful and humorous online presence, your branding would be inconsistent. Similarly, if you want to communicate that you're an experienced real estate agent with a lot of knowledge in the market, you should demonstrate your authority by posting blog posts instead of funny videos and memes.

CHAPTER THREE

BUILDING YOUR SOCIAL MEDIA AND BUSINESS PRESENCE

The secret to winning the real estate game isn't having the best properties at the best prices, this does help, however, to win the game, you need to be discovered. As I stated previously in the book, the real estate market is filled with people trying to stake their claim to their piece of the pie with more and more trying to take that pie every day.

For this reason, you must constantly be looking for new and innovative ways to become discovered and ensure that what you have done in the past, is still visible. This is a full-time job in itself, so creating a powerful team will go a long way in this process.

So far in this book, we talked about carving out your niche, finding the prospects and people you want to connect with and more. Now, with the power of social media and the Internet, you need to learn where they are, why they are there, and ensure that they are ready to hear your message. To do anything less will result in no results or results that give you no sales.

What does this mean?

This means that if you are trying to sell a house, you need to be in the areas where people are looking for houses to buy and are hitting their pain points to get their attention. If you are trying to sell houses that are for young couples looking to start families, then you may want to advertise in groups and other areas that are close to schools, parks and other amenities. If you are looking to sell homes to seniors or people looking to become empty nesters, then you want to focus your efforts in these areas.

When it comes to creating a social media presence, there isn't a one size fits all approach. Each person will need to play to their strengths in this regard. Don't try to sell a house to a sixty-year-old person looking to retire in a community that has twenty year old's looking to party and start families. Knowing where to go in social media is your first task.

Creating your Social Media Strategy

Posting real estate-related content on your Facebook or Instagram account every once in a while, is one thing but having a full-fledged social media marketing strategy that'll yield the results you're looking for is what matters the most!

Here are some suggestions for great information to share on your social media channels: Listings, whether new or current, Team biographies (if you run a real estate brokerage), Case studies, Success stories, and relevant blog entries.

Granted, creating an **effective social media strategy** may be very difficult no matter how experienced you are. However, some tools like Buffer were developed just for that purpose. They're designed to easily aid social media content development and scheduling.

One fundamental rule when developing social media techniques for your real estate business is sharing varied Content. Also, make your Content useful to a broad audience and not just leads who are looking to the market to buy a new home. Both buyers and sellers should benefit from what you put out

Identify the Best Real Estate Social Media Networks

We're getting closer. Now that you have a strategy in mind and a good idea of what works, you need to figure out where you want to post.

Each social media platform requires different resources and strategies to get good results from your posts. They each have several routes of social media marketing for real estate, and each one takes time and money. By being able to choose the media networks that would be best for your business, you ensure that your efforts and resources are channeled towards maximizing the return on your investment (R.O.I.)

Let's talk about a few of these social media networks and how they best function for your real estate marketing.

Facebook: First, there's Facebook. Facebook stands undisputed as one of the most dominant platforms used for realtor social media marketing. It possesses both the perfect demographic for the industry and great posting and marketing tools. You can set up a page on this platform, join local real estate Facebook groups, and use **Facebook Marketplace** for your real estate business.

Instagram: When one thinks of captivating images, Instagram comes to mind. Naturally, stylish property photos go hand-in-hand with the most popular types of content on Instagram. This platform is quickly gaining traction as the best way for luxury or boutique real estate businesses to advertise. To make great use of this platform, you need an optimized bio and popular **real estate hashtags** in your posts.

Here's a trick for you. There's only one secret to boosting your Instagram presence, and that is getting more engagements per post. The more likes, saves, and comments you earn on a post, the more likely it will appear in user feeds. So, how do you get more engagement? The trick is simply to post engaging captions and not just images.

YouTube: YouTube is also an effective social media. Having a real estate channel on YouTube allows you to show a true sense of the properties and surrounding neighborhoods.

Develop a user-friendly website

Can you remember the times you opened a website only to close it quickly because it just wouldn't load fast enough? Can you recall the disappointment you felt when you had to check something out in a hurry, but it failed to load quickly?

That's the same way your prospects will feel if your website isn't optimized for mobile. With so many links and pictures, realtor websites can sometimes be a web developer's nightmare.

However, as a real estate agent, you can **create a responsive website** that is optimized for mobile surfing with the help of a competent web designer and an understanding of what your clients want.

According to statistics, more than 40% of real estate website views come from mobile devices. In other words, nearly half of all online viewing is done on a mobile device; thus, if your website is not designed to be responsive on mobiles, your clients will be unable to visit your site easily.

If you don't know what that means to your business, you'll be leaving a whole lot of money on the table. Here's what you should do instead.

To provide your clients with the greatest experience possible, your mobile-friendly website should have the following content:

- A list of all new listings
- Content to help them through the home-buying process
- Links to key moving-related services, such as attorneys, movers, and house inspectors.
- Images that are optimized for mobile screens
- A faster loading speeds

In addition, **implement a live chat feature** on your website. Your real estate business is exceptionally people centric. This means that it's important to be available whenever prospects need to ask questions.

Invest in a live chat software as it'll allow people to connect with you 24/7 and schedule appointments even without necessarily speaking directly to you.

if you want to get our done-for-you real estate website & template, check out https://soldouthouses.com/easyfunnel

Invest in SEO

Do you want your website to be at the top of the search engine results so you can gain more visibility? Then you have to implement a very **powerful SEO strategy**!

Sadly, search engine algorithms keep changing every day, and to thrive, you always need to stay updated with these changing algorithms.

As a realtor, spend more time on SEO. Keywords are a key part of SEO as prospects use these keywords to search for information online.

To ensure that you're using the right keywords for your business, always do keyword research and add them to your blog posts and articles.

Other elements of SEO to consider include the following:

- Backlinks
- Social media pages
- Online directories
- Title and meta descriptions, snippets, and readability

The highest-ranked material on Google is between 1,140 words and 1,285 words. Hence, it could be a great idea to **write high-value, long-form Content** regularly.

Content marketing

You can't talk about a responsive real estate website without talking about content marketing. Without valuable Content, a highly responsive, mobile-optimized website is just a huge waste.

Content marketing is a very important part of SEO as it's your best bet to have your website indexed. Website content also **helps to build a reputation** as well as to connect with your prospects.

One of the ways to utilize content marketing is through blogging. A blog is an effective way to level up your SEO, create a positive online reputation, and provide your clients practical advice on purchasing or selling a home or other property.

It may interest you to know that responsive websites with a blog often have 434% more indexed pages, which helps real estate agents achieve better SEO.

You should **write articles, reviews, and guides** to help your prospects, buyers or sellers, make informed decisions. The Content of your website must solve a problem and provide answers for buyers and sellers to their most pressing real estate questions.

Actively Engage with Your Target Audience

Your job isn't done just because you have posted on a platform. There's still plenty of interaction left to do! Being able to continually interact with the online community offers a personal touch and boosts engagement. All this is crucial for visibility.

Make sure to respond to comments on your channels, explore forums, respond to people's queries that are relevant to your industry, and even reach out to potential clients through personal messages. Do your best to **start conversations and build trust** with potential customers.

Listing on Real Estate Listing Sites

As a real estate agent, listing properties on real estate listing sites might just be what you need to be successful.

They're essential because, with them, you can serve both buyers and sellers alike. A full-fledged listing will provide adequate information for both buyers and sellers to consult.

Listings add a lot of **value to the credibility of a Realtor** and satisfy the inquisitiveness of interested property sellers and buyers.

For example, if a buyer visits the page and loves the listings displayed there, he will feel much more confident and secure in approaching the services of the website and the realtor.

Listing sites such as **Zillow, Realtor.com, Trulia and MLS** are amazing places to share those listings. You might want to check them out.

Host A Webinar

For successful digital marketing, real estate agents ought to share all their expertise as it establishes them as an authority and causes lead to want to work with them.

One of the many ways to do that is by utilizing techniques such as **online workshops and webinars**. By doing so, you can reach a large audience while staying relevant in the real estate industry.

One webinar hosting tool that will be of help to you is GoToWebinar. It makes the creation and hosting of webinar events easy. It is also extremely user-friendly from both ends of the operation.

For real estate agents, generating **inbound leads** is a crucial part of business, and how better to do it than by getting your name and expertise out there?

Create Real Estate Email campaigns

It doesn't matter what industry you're in, an email marketing nurturing campaign is an invaluable tool for connecting with new leads and keeping your current clients interested in your service.

It should be noted that emails are considered one of the **most effective real estate digital marketing techniques**. A well-executed campaign will guide potential customers through planned activities based on their buyer profile and past interactions with you.

According to a recent report, it was revealed that up to 86% of consumers would prefer to receive emails.

However, the more pertinent your Content is to your potential or present clients, the more likely they will open the email to read what you have to say.

To always produce the desired results, you must ensure that the Content you put out is relevant to what your audience is looking for.

Virtual tour hosting

The virtual tour hosting strategy is a very successful digital marketing strategy in the real estate industry.

This strategy doesn't just **generate 49% faster revenue** for marketers than non-video users, it also aids customers in streamlining the home buying process as potential clients can have an idea of exactly what a home has to offer.

It's always difficult to purchase a home, and that is why your potential clients need you to help ease the entire process.

Here are a few things to keep in mind to have a successful virtual tour:

- Use the actual footage of the home and not digital illusions
- Ensure that the tour is user-friendly and created in 3D
- Make sure your video is engaging and responsive, both on mobile and desktop

You can follow the following few processes below to achieve that:

- Make new or revised lists.
- Create touching stories.
- Create team bios.
- Write relevant blog posts.
- Share varied Content and listings which are relevant to what your prospects are looking for.

Advertise Smartly

The best way to boost your visibility is to advertise. While it may involve some costs, the fastest way to grow and increase reach is through real estate social media advertising by using Google, Facebook, LinkedIn, and Instagram ads that can generate new clicks to the website as well as to your social media.

An effective advert attracts interested people to your business by factoring in location, interest, and likelihood of conversion. This also keeps uninterested clicks or people from your site. The key is to run an ad that offers value and actually makes someone want to learn more.

Set it up to capture their contact information so you can add them to your database to nurture them. Also, utilize engaging calls to action like "Fast selling homes under $X" OR "FREE home selling consultation" to spike interest.

Analyze, Optimize, and Repeat

Now, we're at the final and most crucial part of this marketing plan. You've put in all this work, and now what? Well, now is the time to figure out what's working and to filter out what's not. This is why data **measuring your progress on social media is important**.

It demonstrates if and how your efforts and resources are delivering the expected results. Then, you can tweak your social media marketing plan accordingly to optimize your marketing potential.

Create a Sales Funnel

In real estate marketing, a funnel is a system that you've established to guide prospects online into becoming paying clients. An **effective digital marketing funnel** nurtures these leads until they are ready to either buy or sell, regardless of the stage they are at when they get into your pipeline.

For an effective funnel, you have to create content to fit the different stages of your prospects. Multiple marketing channels are used for prospecting as it allows you to connect to the buyers and sellers at different points.

For example, in the "**Attract channel** ", you ought to create more educational content which will identify you as a real estate expert and start a conversation that'll invariably lead to building customer relationships.

The "**Engage channel**" is used to show why you are the best fit for solving the real estate needs of your prospects. Here, you have their attention, and so, you must build the know, like, and trust factor of your brand.

The "**Delight channel**" has to do with delivering excellent service and providing a 5-star customer experience that'll make the seller or buyer, not just a client but also an advocate for your brand.

Pay-per-click advertising

Pay-per-click advertising, also known as PPC, is a digital marketing strategy popularly integrated by real estate agents who are seeking potential clients that may genuinely be interested in their offering,

It is an amazing method for realtors trying to **create new leads through advertisements** to pay for each time the ad is clicked on.

Pay-per-click ads are used for the direct targeting of potential leads, and unlike other forms of ads, it has a significant benefit that makes them unique.

The main benefit of PPC ads is that you are not charged until someone clicks on your ads. Marketers **average over 2.47% conversion rate with AdWords**, according to research.

With PPC ads, the algorithm usually targets prospects who have previously searched for terms related to the service you're offering using Google or any other similar search engine.

Before getting into PPC advertising, make sure that you have all of your components in place to get maximum value. Simply throwing money at ad's won't get you results. You want to have all of the other components in place before you go and start spending money.

When you do start spending money, start with a small budget. You want to spend as little up front on as many ad variations as you can. So, a good rule of thumb is to start with two or three hundred dollars and create two ads. You want to throw five dollars a day at them for a week or two. Once you start to see results you can see which is the winner and which is the loser.

For the winner, you want to use this as the control ad. This means that you will take that ad, change one thing and then run the ads again. You will then get a clear winner and a loser. Repeat this process for five to ten ads, pitting one against the other for a week or two.

You want to endure that you give each ad enough time to do its thing and get good results. The longer you run your ads the more likely you will find your winner and loser. Don't assume just because one did well out the gate that it is the winner. More often than not, it is a false positive.

Take your time with paid advertising. It is a long game that when done right can bring you in more money than you ever paid into it. However, the opposite is true as well. Throw money at a bad ad and you will become broke faster than you can imagine.

If you want to save time and money building a salesfunnel ,You can get our done-for-you sales funnel package at https://soldouthouses.com/easyfunnel/

104 Real Estate Social Media Post Ideas for Realtors to Generate More Leads Online

Now that you have been introduced to social media and what you can do to get noticed, I have compiled a listing of 100 Social Media Post Ideas that you may want to try. These ideas are just a tip of the iceberg, and you should look for fun and interesting twists on these ideas for your own business.

One thing that you don't want to do is copy what others are doing. When you copy what others are doing and don't really stand out, you won't be noticed. This is the time to be flashy and professional. Look for a pain point and a need that only you and your ream can fill. Then, create your posts speaking to that audience with that twist.

1. A More Personal Post

People always love it when they see some posts that give them a glimpse of your personal life now and then. if you have reached a **significant milestone or a big achievement**, don't hesitate to share it. Share some nice photos if you are going on a vacation.

Did you sell your first 50 properties? Are you celebrating your 10th anniversary as a realtor? All these milestones are worth sharing for the whole world to see.

2. Appreciation Event for Your Clients

If you are planning to throw a non-exclusive **appreciation event** for your clients, don't waste the chance to showcase it on all your social media platforms. Don't forget to share fun photos after the event is over.

3. Business or Partnership Spotlight

Have you joined forces with a local business? Is there a local business you want to highlight? Create a real estate social media post and snap some photos with everyone involved. You can also try doing something a little bit less formal.

As a realtor striving to become the number one go-to local expert, one of the most effective ways to boost your perception as a trusted professional is to reach out to owners of local professionals and have them featured in one of your **real estate social media posts**.

You can try adding a short blurb about their offered services, their service hours and address, and maybe a quick interview with the owner. It is even better if some of the local businesses provide products or services related to home improvement.

4. Buying Anniversary of a Past Client

Commemorating the buying anniversary of the home of a past client is an amazing way to make them feel how much you value them. They will love to remember that day and at the same time if gets you the chance to put your name right before their circle.

5. Closing a New Deal

Closing a deal is a happy milestone not only for your clients but also for you. After all, both of you worked hard on closing on the property. To make this realtor social media post more unforgettable, you can include some details about the new house, the transaction, or the clients themselves, as long as they agree to it.

6. Events at Your Local Community

Part of being a realtor is being updated with the **events happening in your local community**. You can reinforce your personal as a local expert and professional by sharing information and details about these events.

7. Fun Holiday

Every year, there is always one fun holiday that always makes you smile. Sharing something lighthearted on your real estate social media post, with a carefully chosen joke, is a great way to encourage engagement.

8. Contests

Sponsoring giveaways or contests is just the kind of realtor social media post that is guaranteed to get lots of attention. After all, who can say no free stuff, right? There are lots of different types of contests that you can run so you can engage your followers or subscribers.

From those who can pull off the most eye-catching **DIY home renovations**, who grows the most colorful flower garden, or who has the cutest family pet, these contests all spur engagement.

As for the prizes, it can be something as small and simple as gift cards, a cash prize, or other stuff relevant to your contest. Your imagination is the limit here.

9. Giving Back to the Community

If you are like most realtors, you probably take time to help out and give back to your community. You can share about the organizations and causes you care about to show potential leads your commitment to make the place better.

10. Helpful Tidbits of Information or News

Establish yourself as the number one go-to resource for your clients looking for helpful information and news. It can be some **selling or buying details or information about the local area**. You can also highlight a few good news in your local area. Share the newest feel-good story relevant to the local real estate market.

11. Highest Value Listings

Is there anyone who hasn't even imagined what it feels like to live in a sprawling mansion? Grabe this chance to feature your area's most expensive listings. People always love to look at listings with the highest price tags, even when they know it is out of their budget. However, linking from your site to this listing is a great way to attract more people to your website and encourage them to browse through your listings. Encourage your followers to imagine what and how it would feel like to actually live in that property.

12. Information on the Local Housing Market

Always remember that you are a realtor, which means you should be showing people **how well-versed you are in the industry** and the local market trends. Posting housing market information on your social media helps you build credibility and expertise.

13. Just Sold

It is probably one of the most common real estate social media posts that some people just ignore. However, they can actually work wonders if you pair it with the closing's story, particularly if it helped your client fulfill a dream or it was a hard property to sell.

14. New Addition to Your Team

Did your team welcome a new member recently? A real estate social media post can also let your followers get to know more about the member. **Introduce the new member of your team** and share some of the qualities and traits they bring with them.

15. New Property Listings

Share some key exciting details about your up-and-coming listing that will soon hit the market. Add a touch of personality to it by sharing your personal perspective about the property.

One of the most common mistakes that many realtors tend to make on social media is how they love using it as just another place for dumping their listings. It is not a good idea since social media's real value lies in facilitating your social interactions. It allows you to talk directly to people, establish relationships, and make your personal brand more trustworthy.

However, it doesn't mean you can just share some listings every time you please. Listings should never be over 10% to 15% of all your real estate social media posts and prioritize those listings that are notably good deals.

16. Open Houses

Are you hosting an open house for your new listing? Make a quick realtor social media post that your followers can share easily to boost the number of attendees. Highlight all perks such as your co-host and the spread you have prepared.

17. Put the Spotlight on Employees

Is there an employee in your team who always goes out of his/her way to help or assist clients? A realtor social media post that **puts the spotlight on your employees** will make people get to know more about your team and see how much you appreciate them. Talk about the milestones and successes that a member of your team has just achieved recently.

18. Selling or Buying Goals

Remind your social media followers that you are the person they can count on to meet their goals, whether it is for buying or selling. It is also the best chance to remind people that you can also help their referrals.

19. Special Occasions

Is someone in your office celebrating his or her birthday? Use this chance to remind them how great they are as a team member and a person. Documenting such milestones on your realtor social media post is something that followers always love.

20. Testimonials from Clients

While a real estate social media post where you brag about yourself is a no-no, you can always let your clients do it on your behalf instead. Let them share with others how you helped them throughout the deal, and let this testimonial strengthen your brand and build trust among prospective clients.

While you are at it, highlight glowing testimonials from clients to increase your social proof. These client testimonials are **proof of your skills** as a real estate professional, making it easier for your followers to trust you even more.

21. Quote

You might have noticed how people love sharing quotes on social media, specifically Facebook. You see these on everyone's news feeds. So why not try creating one that uses your branding that others can share? Just make sure you don't go overboard with sharing quotes, or you risk losing their impact.

22. What Sets Your Team Apart from the Rest

If you and your whole team achieved a remarkable feat, let others know **why your team is distinct from the rest**. Show the world what makes you different in the first place. However, avoid coming off too braggy and let the team's hard work shine through instead.

23. New Recruitment

If you are looking for a new realtor to be part of your team, don't hesitate to tell potential candidates why they should even be excited about the thought of being part of your team.

24. Say Thank You

Realtors are usually the recipient of kindness and assistance from other community members and businesses. Every time you receive a gift or any help, a **simple thank you** can go a long way as a realtor social media post.

25. Blog Post

Cross-promotion of your other marketing efforts is always imperative. It is also a must to direct people to your site anytime you can. See to it that you install Google Analytics on your site's blog to make it easier for you to track visitors as well as their behavior.

After you have finished writing your newest masterpiece of a blog, don't hesitate to **share this on your social media profile**. Take note that sharing your entire article is not required here.

It is actually better if you don't do so. You can simply use a short synopsis of your blog, pair it with a relevant image and share the link to the full article that your viewers can click on.

26. Animals

Animal photos always get the highest number of social media shares, and this is for a good reason. You can try sharing adorable photos of your pets or someone else's like your neighbor or even your client.

You can also make your post related to real estate if possible. But if not, it is perfectly fine, too.

27. Answer Buyer and Seller FAQs

Show off to everyone your expertise in the real estate field by inviting your subscribers or followers to pose their own questions related to the field and make sure you **answer them right away**.

28. Request for Feedback on the Staging of One of Your Listings

Share your recently staged property and ask people for honest feedback. It will allow you to gain valuable feedback and then **showcase your skills** in staging. At the same time, you can also let your subscribers know how you really care about your staging and its overall quality.

29. Raise Questions

Are you curious to know how your followers feel about the newest development in your area? Why not ask them, then? Doing so can result in an interesting discussion as well as other exciting opportunities to be perceived as the leading go-to expert in your locality.

30. Company Events or News

See to it that people know it when you are attending a company. This kind of post can establish your expertise and prestige. If possible, you can include other team members and tag them using your personal account.

It is also the time for you to share a bit about **why you love to work for your company**. You can also try sharing other interesting developments taking place in your company, such as new charity drives, new training programs, a new picnic, and others.

31. Quiz or Poll

Quizzes and polls are very popular across social media platforms. You won't even be hard-pressed to find quizzes for just about everything and anything under the sun.

These polls and quizzes drive high levels of engagement and offer people lots of excuses to procrastinate whatever they are doing. It makes it a good idea to also **create your own poll or quiz**. It can be a simple fun activity for your followers or a chance for them to grow your current contact database by offering poll results or quiz answers in exchange for their full names and email address.

Depending on the specific poll or quiz you make, you can even gain a deeper insight into what really drives your audience as well as how you can better serve them in the future.

32. Fun Fact

A fun fact is always a great way of breaking up all those real estate talks, and they work almost every time. People love reading and even sharing fun facts.

33. Local Market Listing

Sharing a listing of your competitor that you love is a great chance to help one of your current clients. People always like seeing hot listings, and for all you know, one of them might be interested. Link these to your site listings and share listings from various brokerages and agents.

34. Local Throwback Thursday

It is always amusing to see old photos of your local area. Most of these pictures are also part of archival projects, making them easier to find so you can use them with no need to worry about copyright. You can provide some context for the photos if possible or give an approximate or exact year. It is also fun seeing side-by-side comparisons of the changes that the area has been through.

35. Memes

Facebook is now filled with memes and the good news is that there are also fun ones related to real estate that you can share with everyone in your circle. Memes are a great way to remind others about what you do in a non-pushy, approachable, and humane way. When it comes to memes, all you have to do is have fun!

36. Schedule Regular Giveaways

Rather than just hosting a single event once, you can try to schedule a bi-monthly or even a monthly giveaway. It can be something simple as branded shirts, gift cards, event tickets, and others. You can also **partner up with a local business** to make it possible and advertise to your respective circles of influence alike at the same time.

37. Gifs

Just like memes, everyone also loves to share gifs on social media. Why not share with your subscribers some funny gifs related to your local area or those that are like inside jokes?

38. Post Photos of Neighborhood Highlights, Features, and Amenities

Every time someone buys a new house, they are also buying the new neighborhood in one way or another. Why not highlight several of the **most notable features** that the neighborhood of one of your listings has to offer? Does your area have a new public garden, athletic field, or dog park? Share it, too!

39. Real-Life Work

There is always something fascinating about seeing how people work and go about their real life. And since a realtor like you often works crazy hours and from different places, why not show people what you are doing in your real estate social media post?

You can snap a photo of your workspace, whether it is your home, office, park, or coffee shop. Tell people about the cool places you visit and cool things you see as a realtor.

40. Retweet Local News

Grab the retweet local news, specifically those that are related to real estate, and the effect of the news on the local community. Local news can be easily found on Google News, or you can also visit a local TV news website or newspaper.

The local news stories can also inspire the blog posts that you can also share on your social media platforms later.

41. Life Milestones of a Client

Did one of your clients tie the knot recently? Is the client expecting a new baby soon? Did the client sell their old house and buy a new one?

Share all these stories on your social media platform. Of course, do so only after you ask permission from them.

42. Personally Created Videos

If you are into **content marketing**, why not share your recently created video? This video can be a first walkthrough of the property. It can also be a vlog answering a question on commercial real estate. It can also be some short highlights of the recent real estate training you attended.

43. Open House or Home Showing Video Recap

Due to the pandemic, virtual open houses have almost become a necessity and not just a mere luxury. Have you successfully pulled off a **virtual open house** a few days ago? Post a video recap of the event on your different social media channels. It can be a recap video of the entire event itself or a walkthrough of the property.

44. Videos of Other People

Share someone else's informative or fun video about real estate that you know your subscribers will enjoy. The video can be from a home stager, a real estate coach, or an unusual or funny news story.

45. Supported Charitable Causes

Let your subscribers see your charitable side and bring more attention to a cause you personally support. Most social networks today even let you make a donate now button. It allows you to automatically create charity drives, making it a win-win situation.

46. Success Story of a Client

Everyone loves reading success stories, especially now when the internet and other forms of media are filled with nothing but bad news. A good idea for a real estate social media post is a story about **how your client successfully got their dream home with your help**. Once again, just make sure that you ask permission from your client and take lots of photos of the whole process.

47. Your Own House

If you are currently in the process of selling or buying your own house, why not discuss it with your clients? It is the best time to make them relate to you and the emotions they feel when they sell and buy their own home. Document the whole process and share details about your decision in selling or buying your home.

48. Recurring or Weekly Series

Why not write a series of articles that discusses a particular topic? You can **share each article per week** while hyping the upcoming article in the meantime.

49. Free Activities in Your Local Area

Does your local area have any festivals soon? Are there interesting landmarks that people should see and check out? Are there nice biking trails nearby with good scenery? List down all free activities in the area and share them with your social media followers.

50. Home-Buying Tips for First-Time Buyers

Buying your first home can be very exciting but scary at the same time. To ease their fears and answer their questions, share a **few tips**

for getting the best deals for first-time buyers. You can also add a call to action that will direct your prospects to the landing page where a first-time buyer's guide is waiting for them to download.

51. Inspiration for Home Decoration

Curate your own photos of home decoration inspiration on Pinterest and share the boards on your different social media platforms.

52. Infographics

Infographics give you a chance to pack tons of information into one attractive image. These are also great to be shared on your social media platforms and send some traffic to your site.

As a real estate agent, there's a need to give out information that is engaging for your clients. One of the ways to get this done is through infographics.

Infographics help to **communicate real estate concepts to prospects** which in turn leads to an increase in traffic in whatever medium you're using to share the information, like blogs, for example. It also helps to impress your clients and position yourself as a leader in your niche.

By creating easy-to-understand infographics, both buyers and sellers will be able to understand some of the more technical side of real estate, like bidding, loans, and negotiations.

With the right real estate CRM tools, custom surveys, or case studies, you can be enlightened on the type of questions your audience has so you can create infographics based on what they actually want to know.

Infographics are a very versatile type of visual in real estate. They can be used to summarize processes, compare information, simplify complex topics, and show trends over time. If you're not using it yet, you should jump on it!

53. Customer-Created Content for Community Building

If any of your clients offer a service or product or have an online store, you can also feature it on your realtor social media post.

54. Renovation and Design Tips

Homeowners constantly search for new ways to increase the value of their property or turn it into a comfier environment. You can help them with this by **sharing a few renovation and design tips** so they can boost their home's value in no time.

55. Seasonal Home Tips

Every new season brings a new opportunity to update wall colors, spruce up for an upcoming holiday, or just give your living room a quick revamp. Share a few of your favorite ideas for home decoration for every holiday or season.

56. Special Offers and Discounts

Do you have some special promotions? Don't forget to remind your followers and subscribers about your **ongoing special offers and discounts**.

57. Local Events You are Attending or Hosting

Many major cities have their own official websites where upcoming events are advertised. Take a look at them, look for the most interesting ones, and inform your viewers about them. Things are even better if you are directly hosting or attending some of these events.

58. DIY Home Improvement Projects

With DIY being on the rise, this is the perfect time for your followers to do a few **DIY home improvement projects**. You can show them how you do projects yourself and share some helpful tips in the process.

59. Create a Carousel

Many social networks offer their users the opportunity to create image carousels. You can use these for telling longer stories by displaying an ad with multiple parts or images.

60. List of Big-Box Grocery Store Alternatives and Farmer's Markets

Farmer's markets are the best places where you can find the freshest groceries available in town. You also help your local economy when you promote the farmer's markets in your local area.

61. Content from Local Influencers and Experts

Partner with local influencers and experts and share a few of their content. It works especially well when you sign an agreement with them so they can also share your content.

62. National Industry News

Had the interest rates decreased recently? Are there new programs from the government that simplify the process of getting a mortgage?

Share national industry news to your subscribers so they can stay updated with the latest developments.

63. Grab the Attention of Current and Past Clients with "@ mentions"

You can try to @ mention a client whenever appropriate or possible. Doing so will **encourage them to share your post** and at the same time, you can also have direct interaction with your client.

64. Thank You Note

Using social media to express your gratitude can help you endear yourself to your followers and urge them to reciprocate.

65. Fun Fact about Real Estate

You can also share some interesting facts about your local area's real estate market. These fun facts are always amazing to read.

66. Motivational Quote

These motivational quotes may sound a bit cheesy at times, but they continue to be popular, attracting lots of website traffic, likes, and shares.

67. Trivia About Your Local Area

Share some trivia related to your area, what makes it unique, and the landmarks, museums, and monuments found there. These can also include some interesting animals, vistas, or plants that can never be found anywhere else.

68. Historical Photos of Your Area

Before and after photos are always eye-catching, **adding some sense of pride** to your entire community.

69. Feature Your Most Popular Blog Posts

If any of your blog posts get the greatest number of shares or bring a lot of traffic to your site, you can also feature them again on your social media pages.

70. Recommended Books

You can share your list of the top ten **recommended books to read.**

71. Home Exercising Ideas

You can also use your real estate social media post on how to stay active even in the comforts of the home.

72. Staging Ideas

You can share some strategies you can follow to make your properties look amazing when staging them.

73. Hottest Smart Home Appliance

You can share a photo, video, and short review of the newest must-have smart appliance you can get for your home.

74. Advice on What NOT to Buy

Present a few of the most **common pitfalls buyers should know** and avoid when looking for and buying a new house.

75. Reuse Content from Other Social Platforms

You don't always need to come up with a brand-new realtor social media post for every platform every time. You can try to cut up some of your content on Instagram and turn it into TikTok or you can also stitch together a few shorter videos and use them as a post for Instagram.

76. Break Down the Reputation and Personality of the Different Neighborhoods You Serve

One of the main deciding factors in whether someone chooses to live in a certain neighborhood is none other than lifestyle. Pick some posts to delve deeper into the unique characteristics of every neighborhood you serve.

77. Create and Share a Calendar of Events

Create a simple and clear calendar and share this with your followers if you got some specific **social media events** you want to host such as virtual showings, contests, and Lives. Your followers can then make the necessary plans to participate in your events.

78. How much ($$$) Will Get You in (Insert City)

This is among the most consistently searched and viewed topics on social networks filled with visuals. It is understandable because the price is usually the **number one deciding factor** as far as real estate is concerned.

79. Inspire New Realtors

Can you still recall all the content you read up when you were getting started as a realtor? Broaden your circle of influence by posting some relevant content and serving as a reliable resource for real estate students.

80. Interview Clients

Talk to your clients directly on live videos to give insights to your potential clients on what to expect.

81. Invite a Professional Guest

Is there a real estate-related expert in your area that wants to share some helpful advice? You can ask an appraiser, local plumber, insurance representative, or other experts if they have advice for home buyers and create a shareable post about them.

82. Gardening and Landscaping Ideas

First-time home buyers are often first-time garden owners as well. Help them by **offering gardening tips** to help them beautify the exterior of their homes.

83. Lifestyle Content

Do millennials who live in the city center make up the most of your clients or followers? Do you cater more to large families relocating to the suburbs? You can **share some lifestyle tips** relevant to them in their new neighborhoods.

84. Make Saveable Checklists

Moving involves a long list of steps and processes. Come up with helpful checklists your followers can save or view on your page.

85. Post Before and After's

A before and after is a great way of showing clients how they can improve their properties to increase their value.

86. Repost Relevant Influencers

Reposting your favorite relevant influencers or even doing a duet with them is a great way of hopping on a famous trend and sparking post engagement.

87. Share Tricks You Use in Your House

Realtors like you are some of the people in this world who have seen a lot of homes in their lifetime. This means you have already tested and gathered a few tips that your prospective clients may find helpful.

88. Throwback Posts

People always love flashbacks to fonder days. It doesn't matter if it is a **flashback post about your professional achievements or personal life**, a peak of the past will surely gain attention.

89. Interior Design Trends

You might have noticed some constant interior design trends among your latest property listings. You can share these with your clients who might not have personally viewed many homes.

90. "Home of the Week"

Home of the week can be an inspirational area of the house that suits your style or even a recent sale.

91. Contact Information

While your website may already have it, give your subscribers that extra push to call you by using your real estate social media post to remind them.

92. Favorite Podcasts

An informative and entertaining podcast is an effective and **easy way to effortlessly gain tidbits of helpful information**.

93. Day-in-the-Life

Show your followers what happens in your day as a realtor.

94. Use New Social Media Features or Filters

Take advantage of the newest features and filters so you can increase the success and reach of your posts.

95. Real Estate Terms Made Simple

While all **real estate jargon** may already be familiar to you, these may sound like alien words to your clients. Sharing a handy vocabulary word with its definition now and then can offer your followers some value.

96. Free Resources

Clients often research every single detail of the process of buying a property. You can help them out by sharing free resources.

97. Seasonal Tips

Every season brings new concerns and demands. Keep your subscribers in the loop all year long.

98. Tell Your Story

Authenticity and humanity are what make any profession appealing. **Share your personal stories** that made you learn a lesson you want to share with your followers.

99. Experience the Property

Generate buzz about your property listing by making a post about what it feels like to spend an average day at a particular property.

100. Behind the Scenes

Behind-the-scenes content can build anticipation about your new listing. Take some BTS content if you have stagers, videographers, and other service providers visiting the property. Post the content on your social media for your followers to see the **hard work spent just to sell a property**. It will make them curious to see the result.

101. Real Estate Terms

Another way to generate leads through social media posts is by making posts about real estate terms.

Most buyers and sellers have little understanding of those terms and would love nothing more than to have them explained to them for free. But that's not all. It positions you as an expert in their minds and helps them trust you and eventually become your clients.

Any realtor who is wanting to get inbound leads must leverage creating content on real estate terms.

102. Real Estate FAQ

For both sellers and buyers, the process of buying or selling a house is a very challenging one, especially if you don't have the experience. Real estate transactions are very complicated, so it's quite normal to have a lot of questions during every step of the buying or selling journey.

With prospects lying in wait with countless questions on their minds, making posts that answer these questions is a powerful way to build trust and credibility and convert these prospects into leads.

For example, you can ask questions like:

- Are real estate commissions negotiable?
- How much does a seller pay in closing costs?
- How can a real estate agent help me sell a home?

Answers to questions like these will help you generate leads for your real estate business.

103."Just Sold" Post

Anyone who wants to sell a property would love to meet a real estate agent who knows how to sell houses and not one who just claims to. This is where this kind of post comes in.

"Just sold" posts demonstrate to your prospects that you have what it takes to help them either buy the house of their dreams or sell their house. It works even better if you incorporate a story, as it humanizes your brand and helps your prospects connect with you.

Was it difficult to sell the home? Did the sale help your client fulfill their dreams? Posts like that help to generate leads. Yet, you must do it well. **Here's an example:**

Peter got an unexpected job transfer in March and suddenly had to move and leave his home. He was worried about selling his home from 2,500 miles away, especially in the dead of winter in an area where homes usually take months to sell. It took a bit of unconventional marketing, but Peter's home sold in just a few months for $700,000, which enabled him to buy his new dream home. All the best to him!

Posts like this allow prospects to see themselves and crave the same results as the person in the post. You should try it.

104."Just listed" Posts

If you want to hype up your new listings, the best way is to post about them so that everyone can see them.

Don't just do it once. Come on, don't be shy. Go on and share them repeatedly. Your entire audience can't see it each time, so reminders and multiple shares will maximize its reach.

Share a few details about the house, post pictures of different angles and areas and, of course, inject some personality into it.

Be sure to **include an exterior shot** and a few of the **best interior shots**, like the most important details, the number of beds and baths and very importantly, include a link to the listing on your website.

105.Testimonials

We know that high-quality pictures may attract new leads, but you need testimonials to sell them. Many people may only choose you as their realtor if they can see that you've done a great job for others.

Bragging about yourself matters very little. No one cares about that. But when others brag about you, it means the whole world! Let them tell others how helpful you were during their **real estate transaction**. This is the best way to build trust with potential clients.

If it's long, don't post the entire testimonial. People don't have the time. Instead, post a few lines and then link to the full post on your website.

Don't just post text, people can easily gloss over it. Add some graphics to it; perhaps, a nice photo. **There are a few vital things you must note when posting testimonials:**

- Mention the client's name and city.
- Tag the client in the picture from your personal account so that their friends can see it, too.
- Don't post them too often. Make it seem natural. Ensure that they're broken up with plenty of other posts.

These are just a few ideas for your social media marketing. There are countless others that you can try to do and work into your business. Don't be afraid to try something new and to go at your message from a totally different angle. When you get someone looking at you for one thing, then you slip in something else, they will usually say, "I didn't know you could do that."

This is where we get the know you, like you and trust you factors in marking and promotion. Find ways for people to know who you are, like what you do and what you stand for and trust you by giving them something of value. This is the secret of marking and social medial.

if you want to save time and money on creating those social media content yourself, check out our done-for-you social media post package at https://soldouthouses.com/365doneforyoucontent

CHAPTER FOUR

BUILDING LEADS AND GETTING CLIENTS

Now we are at the point where all of your bard work and dedication will start to pay off. When you start getting emails, phone calls and text messages from people, these are known as your leads. It is important that you follow up with all of these leads in a specific order and timely manner. If you get a lead and you wait a week to get back to them, then they may have found a solution somewhere else, their needs may have changed, or they just don't want to deal with you.

The rule of thumb is to have all of your leads funneled into some type of call center or office where you have dedicated people to answer calls, emails and texts. Their job is to get on the phone with your leads as soon as they come in so they can try to move them down your sales funnel or get them into a consultation call where you can talk one on one and work your magic. Failure at this point in the process will mean failure. You can't go any further if you don't nurture your leads.

Building a relationship with Local Businesses

Creating mutually beneficial alliances with insurance companies, personal bankers, lenders, nearby hospitals, bakeries, hardware stores, and so on, and also trying to co-host events that will help both parties to attract typical clients is one of the best ways to generate quality leads.

You can also use this avenue to **provide discounts to clients** who use referred connections so that you and your partners can cultivate leads for mutual growth.

Attend trade shows and expos

Local or global events and tradeshows are excellent venues for showcasing your real estate projects and raising awareness of your company's name and brand.

In order to generate leads during these events for your real estate property, all you need is to communicate with potential buyers or partners, distribute flyers, and pitch your offerings.

You may also get the chance to meet with industry professionals and learn about the **newest and emerging trends**. It is also one of the greatest ways you can use to generate leads.

Host open houses

Open houses continue to be a popular way to get Real Estate Leads. This might be as easy as hosting an open house for the house you are selling.

To get the most out of open houses, do the following to attract the attention of potential buyers and their real estate professional representatives:

- Ensure that guests sign in, and place your open house sign-in station just outside the entrance, and include lots of additional sign-in forms and pens.

- In the weeks leading up to your open house, run specific **open house advertising and promote your property** widely. Have the home advertised at least five days before the open house.

- Remember that real estate signage and sign riders are efficient techniques to create interest and business. On the day of the event, wake up early and **distribute signs with the open house schedule** around the neighborhood.

- Make a real effort to learn what clients are seeking and demonstrate why the house meets those criteria.

Real Estate Framing

Framing is an effective way of generating leads in real estate. In framing, you'll present a piece of information in a way that'll make your prospects react the way you want them to, thereby increasing your conversions.

As a real estate agent, you can make use of either positive framing, which focuses on what the prospect stands to gain, or negative framing, which taps into their natural fear of losing out on something. Either way, you're trying to get them to make the decision you want them to make.

Many may consider **real estate postcard marketing** to have gone out of fashion, but even today, postcards are effective in generating leads. Pulling on every string you have in such a competitive industry is important. Making use of a multichannel marketing approach to reach your target audience in different locations gives you an edge.

Many agents are aware that direct mailing is important for lead generation, but only a few makes use of direct mail as a marketing tactic. With real estate postcards, you have an effective marketing tactic for generating leads and building brand awareness. They can also be used for follow-up communication, upcoming listings, just-sold properties, open houses, and more.

These real estate postcards are often only 5×7 inches in size and should be designed to be very attractive to clients. It's always a great idea to incorporate a **positive customer review** on your postcard and even to sometimes use humor to get your message across. However, it is important to remember to use the 'less is more" mindset with your designs.

We advise that you keep to a minimalist design as much as possible. Make sure it includes your logo, contact information, and more details about your business on the reverse side. See the description below or visit https://soldouthouses.com/pro/ to learn more about our real estate Postcard Templates.

Work With the Right Brokerage

One of the first and most important decisions you'll make as a new real estate agent is the brokerage you'll work for. Your brokerage will determine whether **you gain experience in your industry**.

In all honesty, many real estate brokerage firms are waiting to hire you. However, not all of them are good for you. In fact, one of the leading reasons why real estate agents fail is because they lack the right training and support in their first two years.

So, how do you ensure that you get the right brokerage to work for?

Firstly, do a lot of research. You want to identify a brokerage that shares the same goals and values as you. You're more likely to succeed with such a firm.

Secondly, book interviews with multiple brokerage firms. While you'll carry along your real estate certification and prepare to answer some questions, don't forget that this is also your chance to get to know the firm. The interview is just as important for you as well.

Ask specific questions about their needs and goals. See whether these values and goals will launch your career in the right direction.

In case you want to know some pointers that'll help you choose the right brokerage, look out for a firm that:

- Is located in the market you want to work in
- Serves your target clients and the niche you're interested in
- Offers great mentorship and training

Since you're new, focus heavily on training and mentorship. Your first brokerage firm should offer the right support, education, and tools.

Keep in mind that while you can always change your brokerage firm later in your career, you only have this one time to launch it. Make sure you start it well.

Widen Your Sphere of Influence

Real estate deals are greatly reliant on relationships. Your network is the best source for your first clients.

Since you're a beginner, you may not have a wide network at first. That's why you need to use your sphere of influence. While many newbies may think they do not have a sphere of influence, they just don't know how to identify it.

*Your sphere of influence (SOI) includes your family, friends, colleagues, and acquaintances. These are the people who will **help you get your first clients** and help grow your network.*

Have all their details and contacts in one place, such as a spreadsheet, email database, or any commercial software, for easier monitoring. Once you have them in one place, you can then add more contacts each time you meet someone new through your SOI.

The key to having an effective network lies in numbers. The more people you have in your SOI, the greater your chances of getting deals and new clients through referrals.

Invest your time to meet new people and add them to your network. One easy way to do this as a beginner is by attending industry events. Stay in the loop for upcoming workshops, seminars, and any other networking opportunities.

Once you've met new people and gotten their contact information, don't stop there. Ensure they'll keep thinking about you by constantly checking in with them. You want them to remember you and what you do so that they may reach out when they or someone close to them needs your services.

Use the Right Marketing Materials

Once you've obtained your real estate license, you want to ensure everyone knows about it. You increase your chances of bagging your first client by starting to market aggressively sooner.

You can start with marketing basics such as:

- Ordering creative business cards
- Creating an email list

- Taking a high-quality professional headshot
- Having a real estate bio
- Social media presence

Since you're just starting out, note that you don't need to implement every marketing strategy immediately. Marketing is a full-time job that requires you to dedicate a lot of time and resources.

Let's say you decide to create your realtor website and build an audience for your social media pages at the same time. You'll spend a lot of time juggling between both strategies and you'll most likely forget to look for clients.

Have a clear idea of your priorities.

This will help you stay grounded and not get carried away by tasks that don't benefit your core business. Talking to your mentor, team leader, or business coach will help you set your priorities.

Another important marketing tip for new realtors is that you shouldn't shoulder the burden of doing everything by yourself. While you may not have the budget to hire someone else to do some tasks for you, keep in mind that outsourcing is the most efficient way to get things done.

Monitor Your Finances

As I mentioned previously, being a real estate agent isn't the same as being an employee. Here, you're not promised a paycheck at the end of the month. Besides, your taxes won't be automatically deducted on payday. You now have to **track your business revenue and expenses yourself.**

Remember, not all months will generate the same income. Some months will have lower commissions than others. As such, you need to save for a rainy day. You can only save if you monitor your finances.

Budgeting is a tricky affair for most people. It can even become more stressful during tax season. Tracking your finances is a vital skill for all successful realtors. As a newbie, you can start by splitting your business and personal finances. You shouldn't use your personal finances for business affairs and vice versa. **Have separate bank accounts** for each.

Add more separate accounts, business revenue, and expenses. Save all your business receipts and monitor your profits and losses. Also, you can avoid budgeting monthly as most salaried professionals do. Instead, have an annual budget.

Remember, outsourcing is an efficient way to grow your business. You can hire an accountant to maintain your financial books and also pay your taxes on time. You can also **automate the process by using accounting software** to streamline all your financial processes, generate financial reports, and prepare quarterly and annual tax returns.

Market Update

Whether they're buying or selling, people always tend to follow the market closely for a few months at least before deciding to list or make a decision. As a real estate agent, posting statistics about your local market will help you put yourself in front of prospects and keep your existing clients informed.

You can do this using your **local real estate board's monthly or quarterly reports**. The post can either be in the form of a graphic post, a Reel or a TikTok post. These are particularly effective because they're quick to film and are great ways to market yourself showing your own personality and presence.

Posts on market updates will show your prospects that you know your stuff and are well-informed about what's happening in the local market. As a realtor, this is an amazing way to build expertise. Yet, you must be careful not to make it boring, and **I'll show you how in a few steps**.

- Don't just list stats, tell them why those stats matter.
- Use less text.
- Don't use industry jargon. They don't understand that, so they'll simply scroll past.
- Always remember to link to the original source.

Neighborhood News

Everyone loves to know what's happening around them or around the place they wish to move to. Hence, the choices of both buyers and sellers are highly influenced by the neighborhood they're in, or where they want to live.

What does this imply? Any real estate agent should take advantage of this fact and **create content around it to gain leads**. It can be in the form of posting guides or neighborhood stats.

Neighborhood guides are of more importance to buyers relocating to a new city. They'll need to know things about their neighborhood that they can't find on Google. You can make posts in the form of carousel posts, Reels, and TikTok.

Posting statistics for a specific neighborhood helps **attract potential clients wanting to list their home in that neighborhood**. It displays your experience at a micro-local level and gives that client the confidence that you can get them the best results.

It's also valuable information for those looking to buy in the area, giving them an idea of price benchmarks and what to expect.

Create a Visually Stunning Website and Update It to Boost Visibility

For realtors, there is no better way to present listings from the MLS than with an Internet Data Exchange or IDX-enabled website. **The IDX technology can organize fresh MLS listings straight to the site**. It allows leads to view all of your area's available property listings from it.

In addition, some tools also let you visually showcase the latest information and statistics in real estate and provide features such as lead capture forms. It means that as you browse your slides, the prospective lead will be allowed to receive valuable content in exchange for their email.

Pop-up ads are also valuable elements for website design. However, these should be non-intrusive and intuitive enough to avoid annoying potentials. Other features such as client testimonials, blog pages, content upgrade offer, social media links, and community news can help bring your website together as the cornerstone of your real estate marketing strategy.

Aside from creating a visually stunning website, it is also important to **update to increase visibility**. Remember that old blogs tend to get pushed further down on the search engine result page or SERP by Google for many different reasons.

Make sure you stay updated with any content covering time-based events or trends. Updating your site or blog with some valuable content will not only boost your position as an authority or expert in your field. However, it will ultimately boost your visibility in the search results.

Add these elements to your real estate marketing strategy to bring more leads soon!

Use Targeted Landing Pages

You will be able to market something more unique and specific if you create a landing page that is separate from that of your brokerage. Once you have finished developing your landing page, you can drive more traffic to it by advertising or posting it on social media, search engines, and networking groups. Capturing leads can be as simple as creating your own destination page with a call to action and contact form.

Segment Leads to Gain Database Insight

While many of the people who get your newsletters and the rest of your **promotional emails** are leads that already exist in your system, you can organize them according to different criteria to provide you more insight into your database and help with lead generation at the same time.

It is where lead generation can come in handy. Some of the criteria that you can use for segmenting your leads may include the following:

- Demographics by buyer personas
- How cold or hot they are, such as how much they interact with your social media, website, content, and more
- Specific behaviors range from downloading a specific electronic guide or signing up for your mailing list

Once you are equipped with this knowledge, you will be able to tailor the different elements of your outreach for your different segments, including your educational materials, the frequency of contact and nature of your clients, and emails.

Even if hot leads might require a more personalized prod to make them do what you want them to do, cold leads might be better left on email drip. You will reap more benefits and save time or energy if you invest your marketing resources astutely in people who are most likely to buy through segmenting.

Consider a Real Estate Lead Generation Service Subscription

Although it is preferable to use organic and free strategies for lead generation, you can also find companies specializing in real estate lead generation that can help you save time. They can quickly provide you with contact details and names of highly motivated potential sellers and buyers.

Leads will be sent to you via text or email, depending on the specific service you use. These leads may also come one at a time or in batches.

Send Targeted Mailers and Messages

The main focus of targeted mailing are people who meet specific criteria such as high-income households or good credit score.

Similar to newsletters or postcards, **bulk electronic marketing** or mailers are just like text or email messages letting you reach out to more prospective clients compared to what you can by just using networking alone.

Although you can come up with your own targeted list, it is also possible for you to buy a list of addresses from third parties to help hasten the process.

Business cards, flyers, and postcards pinned to the bulletin boards at coffee shops are good examples of a tip for prospecting known as cold canvassing. The process of cold canvassing establishes name recognition that can come in handy for newer realtors who wish to break into a bigger market.

But it is more likely for you to get a lead if your content is tailored according to where it is being sent. For instance, **you can try cold canvassing** some rental buildings in your community with titles and information that will make the wonder why they should rent if they can buy instead.

Postcards might not offer the highest return on investment. However, most brokerages, as mentioned earlier, provide their realtors a specific number of postcards for every deal as an incentive for being part of the firm so it wouldn't hurt to give it a try.

You can use these postcards for announcing that you have become a part of a new brokerage. Postcards may also contain market information or new listing promotion. Don't forget to proofread your postcards and include a headshot as well. Your mailers will only end up in the circular file once your clients see spelling and grammatical mistakes.

Another way to make your mailers count is to **purchase a targeted mailing list** so that you will send them to a particular audience.

Show Generosity in Agent-to-Agent Referrals

Agent referrals happen every time you connect with other agents in different markets using any of your connections. Once you send over a referral to a fellow agent and their deal is closed, you will be paid a certain percentage of the sales commission which is typically anywhere around 25% to 45%.

The same rule is also applicable if you were the one who received a referral, and this time, you will pay the referring agent a percentage as commission. You can use a referral service for this, or you can also make your own connections.

These **agent-to-agent referrals** serve as a great source of relatively passive income. When you send other agents more referrals, it also increases the chances of you getting referral checks every time people close deals.

Get Your Ads Running on Social Media and Search Engines

Paid and free are the two main types of leads that you can integrate into your real estate marketing strategy. But you can expect the highest level of success if your lead generation campaign strikes the perfect balance between these two types. You can use social media and search engines to generate both paid and organic leads. You can also use paid ads to get more results in a short span of time. You can also combine your strategies to ensure long-term results.

To take advantage of your online advertising efforts to the fullest, you have to look at it as something similar to virtual farming where your final goal is establishing your name recognition instead of just selling all leads right away. Having said that, provided that you offer potential customers engaging content, these channels can serve as a great source for lead generation in real estate.

As modern marketing goes digital, your social media image and reputation have already become an indispensable element of any real estate marketing strategy. **Facebook, Instagram, Twitter, and LinkedIn are just some of the top platforms worth your investment**.

LinkedIn is an obvious option as it is more specifically geared to professional networking, while Twitter and Instagram attract the most awareness and traffic. Some Instagram strategies combined with simple and short posts and stunning visuals will keep you accessible and relevant in the daily life of potential clients.

Another cost-effective method for lead generation is **Facebook Ads** which let you target your database's existing leads through the Custom Audiences feature. You can also create a local group on Facebook around your company that will allow your clients to share their experiences and offer new leads a glimpse of what they can expect as homebuyers.

Here are other great lead generation opportunities through online ads:

- **Instagram and Facebook advertising**

You can create ads that will target specific people with special interests, people you want to work with, and geographic areas. Social media can drive more website traffic and your ads can also help you promote upcoming special events. Advertising with Facebook lets you reach people on the News Feed, Messenger, and Instagram stories.

- **Google My Business**

Your details, including your name, link to your website, and phone number will be visible on the right sidebar of the screen of a user's device if you create your business listing with Google My Business that you can use for free.

- **Local community pages**

You can link these dedicated landing pages with IDX or internet exchange data feeds and present for sale properties in a particular target market. It makes these pages a great tool that you can incorporate into your real estate marketing strategy.

- **NextDoor**

NextDoor is a social platform that offers message boards where neighbors can chat about their concerns, discuss local issues, or even look for lost pets. The Neighborhood Sponsorship tool also gives you an opportunity of promoting yourself in pop-up ads while users browse through content for anywhere around $100 to $1,000 monthly.

- **Search engine advertising**

Microsoft Advertising and Google Ads are two of the most popular services that allow keyword targeting and featuring listings at the bottom and top of the SERPs or search engine results pages. It is designed in a way that appears like other search results.

Use SEO to Attract Leads

There are many people in your area at any given time that turns to search engines to look for answers to their questions related to real estate. With a solid **SEO or search engine optimization strategy** in place, you can add your site to search results, address common questions that will showcase your trustworthiness and expertise, and capture more new leads.

Even though SEO is not among the easiest strategies for real estate marketing, this long-term strategy constantly brings you new and highly targeted leads with no need for you to exert a lot of effort and time. It makes SEO an extremely effective lead generation strategy for realtors.

Running a podcast

An effective strategy to interact with your audience and promote to them in non – traditional ways is to run a podcast. It is a powerful tool for marketing your business because it has more than 380 million listeners worldwide.

Using podcasts regularly to engage your audience is an intriguing tactic for holding their attention. By podcasting about real estate and other relevant issues, you will be able to reach out to a large number of potential buyers on a more personal basis, which will eventually benefit your business.

When coming up with podcast subjects, you should search the web for noteworthy **real estate market trends, intriguing news, and blog posts**. There are countless subjects you can discuss; even personal experience-based counsel would be appropriate.

You may occasionally bring on another prosperous agent to your podcasts to share their stories as well. Just make certain that you can thoroughly and accurately explore those subjects so that you establish yourself as an expert. If you want more tools & templates to get more marketing leads, check out the description below or go to Soldouthouses.com.

Guerilla marketing

Guerrilla marketing is the employment of creative, unorthodox strategies to increase sales or spark interest in a product or company.

The element of surprise is key to guerrilla marketing. Realtors need to provide their target markets with unexpected offerings. It captures an audience's attention in ways conventional marketing cannot by adopting unconventional and low-cost techniques.

A lot of conventional realtors still stick to **conventional marketing strategies** because they've been proven to be effective. However, innovative thinking is necessary to establish your brand and differentiate yourself from the competition.

You can hand people business cards in unconventional materials. For example, you could put a business card in an envelope that appears like a shopping voucher and hand it out to people. They'll discover a business card with an invitation to come house-hunt with you when they open it.

You can leverage trending events to make jokes or memes about them, which you can connect to your business. In 2016, a realtor gained notoriety for making a joke out of an American situation which had people threatening to leave the country and relocate to Canada by putting up different billboards and offering to sell the houses of those who were ready to move.

You can pull off any appropriate publicity stunt that'll draw attention to your brand. A compelling piece of content will sell itself since many people will want to share it with their friends and make jokes about it, which will generate publicity. Who knows, it might reach someone who would be interested in your services.

There are no limitations when using **guerilla marketing techniques**. You are completely free to express yourself. You will create a lasting impression on your target audience when used correctly.

One-day lease

It is quite strange that we make decisions almost blindly about a transaction as important as acquiring a house. What we suggest is a **form of Airbnb marketing idea**. The same way you can get a test drive for a car before buying, let potential buyers take the house for "a test day."

Let the family or the person buying spend a night or a day alone, unsupervised, and live in the house like it has already been paid for. Yes, you can attend open houses, walk through a home, and take pictures, but none of these give the entire experience of living in the house.

Of course, you must persuade the sellers to allow the property to be used for a specific time and get their valuables in a safe room or locked up in drawers. You also need some paperwork for a **signed agreement to cover any possible damages** made by the potential buyer.

The current homeowner can make the home available through their own Airbnb account or just simply make it like a listing on your real estate portal. The deal could be to have the buyer spend a night, or a full 24 hours, or even just a morning till the evening of the same day, as long as the current owner agrees. Buying a property is an emotional decision, so offering the opportunity to bond with the house you're about to spend a lot of money on is an offer no one will refuse.

This marketing idea is for a potential buyer who actually is interested and has shown substantial interest in becoming your client.

Running educational webinars

Technology developments have made it possible for real estate agents to reach potential clients in an almost limitless number of inventive ways. Webinars are one of the most engaging and effective.

In general, all facets of the real estate industry, including purchasing and selling, **require some level of credibility and trust** to be built in order to win over potential clients.

Clients looking to purchase or sell their property want a realtor who can exhibit a thorough understanding of the present market and insight into emerging trends. By hosting a webinar, you have a chance to extensively educate them on these topics.

By hosting webinars, you may also **share your unique perspective and solutions** to the most pressing problems your participants will likely face. These problems for sellers include how to price their homes fairly, sell for a profit, or get offers from buyers. For sellers, these problems may include how to successfully negotiate prices, how to stay clear of conveyancing problems, how to find a suitable property, and many other things.

You should be available for queries from the audience during the interactive portion of the presentation so that you can respond and establish your credibility as an experienced and dependable realtor.

Social Media polls

Most social media platforms like Twitter and Instagram now have a feature displayed as "Polls." This feature is an essential tool for you as a real estate agent. It is a quick way to traffic on your page!

Why? We all love to give our opinions on almost everything, even things we sometimes don't know much about.

So, giving your general audience the avenue to vote on things like preferred interior decorations or home structure or even seemingly unimportant stuff like the size of lawn they'd rather have, makes them feel special. **It shows you value their opinion and views**. But more than that, it helps you, as an agent, to understand potential buyers' needs and wants.

From the results of these polls, you can understand customer preferences allowing you to improve your strategy to satisfy a particular audience. Take note to ALWAYS attach your polls to pictures or videos to make them less abstract and more relatable.

You can also get access to our done-for-you social media post templates by clicking on the link below or going to soldouthouses.com to learn more!

Take advantage of infographics

Infographics are pictures that present information in a way that makes it more fascinating to read than typical written text. With the help of **infographic marketing**, a business can present information in a way that stands out from the crowd and differentiates it from rivals.

Using infographics will always be more effective than written texts because infographics are easier to understand. Your audience will be more interested in your content if you creatively represent information using graphs, charts, and tables since people pay more attention to images than to text.

Also, captivating and interesting **infographic content would help your brand go viral**, thereby increasing the number of clients you can attract. People don't always want to read an in-depth explanation of why your product or service is valuable, which is where marketing infographics come in.

In one succinct, captivating visual, you can explain why you are the best realtor or even why your listing is the best in the area. You can click on the description below or visit soldouthouses.com/infographics/ for our 150-done-for-you real estate infographic package.

Posting educational real estate content

It might become really monotonous posting your listings time and again. By **sharing educational materials** on your social media sites, you can display greater creativity. You should keep up with local events in your niche area by reading local newspapers and community events calendars and then posting about them.

Write about local businesses like the markets, stores, restaurants, or other businesses near and in your target area. You can also discuss the area's transportation accessibility, such as which streets or areas have the quickest access to bus stops, train stations, or metro stations.

You could also discuss the local points of interest, such as parks, and list the greatest parks and the activities they provide, such as picnic areas and beaches. You should also share things like market data, neighborhood analyses, **home seller or buyer tips**, and answers to frequently asked questions to establish yourself as an expert.

Creating social media content on these topics will demonstrate your expertise in the real estate industry, which would encourage individuals to use your services.

Repurposing contents

Content creation used to be straightforward because all you had to do was produce a blog, a podcast, or a video and then distribute it to all available social media channels. You can use the **same copy, hashtags, and captions across the board**.

But it's no longer that simple. There are more channels than ever, and there is tremendous competition among them. You must ensure that your content satisfies the requirements for each platform because there are different expectations from the various audiences across the various platforms.

Repurposing content entails reusing content that you already have or are creating and utilizing it to produce social media posts differently. You can accomplish this by breaking up your blog post into an engaging Twitter chat or turning it into a YouTube video.

There are several benefits to using previously developed content again. It gives you a presence, saves you time, and maintains the consistency of your brand. Additionally, it encourages engagement because you are more likely to receive **impressive engagement rates** the more posts you produce.

Organize Quizzes and Contests

Quizzes and contests are very underrated real estate marketing ideas! Create a quiz or contest on your website, post the links about the details, or even the answers to the quiz questions on your social media platform.

Your **quiz questions should be real estate related** but also based on questions random people can have answers to. Try quizzing on topics like 'how much you know your state,' 'identify and name home decorators,' or 'guess the owners of these celebrity houses.' Make sure they have to do with real estate and are not too difficult, so people don't lose interest.

For contests, engage your followers and friends by making contests like the best vegetable garden or the most impressive interior decoration, or who has the cutest family pet. Maybe even simple contests like "Home of the Week"!

No quiz or contest is complete without a prize, but don't worry, you don't have to spend millions to get prizes for winners. From something as simple as maybe a **free consultation session** with a real estate expert to giving out the merchandise of your real estate company like branded t-shirts, mugs, pens, face caps or gift cards. Just make sure your prizes are tangible as well as advertise your business!

Employ humor in your social media campaign

Marketing is said to be effective once it is noticeable and memorable, and according to studies on the **"humor effect,"** hilarious content is more recalled than non-comedic content because people focus more on things that are amusing, which is why we can recall them.

By posting funny content that clicks, a lot of people will know and always remember your brand.

For the obvious reason that people like to laugh, funny memes and videos are shared more frequently than any other kind of content on social media. By incorporating humor in your social media posts, you'd achieve virality which would give you more exposure and drive more sales. Creating humorous content also helps you grab your audience's attention.

There are already too many serious ads out there, so **incorporating the right type of humor** into your marketing campaign will make your business stand out from the others.

CHAPTER FIVE

THE OPEN HOUSE

For most realtors the open house is where you can work your magic. You are there with the prospect, you can walk them through the property, answer questions and so much more. It is here that typically the deal will be struck or at least you will get offers.

To make sure that your open house is a success there are some things that you should really take into consideration, prioritize, and simply avoid all together.

How To Host A Successful Open House

1. Do your research

As a realtor who is planning an open house event, the first step you should take is to do your research. Research opens you up to a lot of information you'll be needing, especially those that could entice your target market to come to your open house event and also convince them that you're a notable realtor. You should be well acquainted with the house as well as the neighborhood. This would help you know selling points to highlight. Things like "This house is 10 kilometers away from this renowned hospital, there's a kindergarten in the next street, there are two relaxation areas, transportation links to major roads plus proximity to any amenity sought after by house hunters.

Also, you should have every information concerning the house because people will ask you, Learn as much as you can about the property, neighborhood, and local housing market. You want to be in a position to answer questions such as:

- how many bedroom apartments is this?
- When was this house built?
- What type of finishing or building materials were used in the building?
- Is it soundproof?
- How long has the home been for sale?
- What's the square footage in the garage?
- What upgrades have been done on the home?
- Does the property have any structural issues?
- Is there a homeowners' association (HOA)?

Ensure you answer these questions appropriately. Don't panic if anyone asks a question you can't answer convincingly. Simply jot down their contact information and promise to get back to them.

Another essential aspect of carrying out due diligence involves conducting a **comprehensive comparative market analysis** (CMA). Since you might end up hosting a few neighbors and residents from nearby, you want to be an authority in the local market. An in-depth

CMA will help you understand the value of such properties, listings that have recently sold, and current listings in that area.

Real estate agents who go the extra mile are more likely to succeed in their careers. Set aside a day to tour a few listings comparable to yours within the neighborhood. Note at least three features that your property has which the comps don't. It could be more square footage, an extra bedroom, or larger storage space. Put yourself in a position where you can quickly point out three features that make your listing unique.

Viewing other comparable properties is also important since you can suggest a few more properties to the potential buyers in case yours isn't exactly what they want. Going the extra mile could make a difference and allow you to **convert a lead into a buyer.**

The more you conduct your due diligence, the higher your chances of hosting a successful open house.

2. Prepare materials

After doing your research and getting the juicy information you need, next All these items should have aesthetic branding. Your **branding as a realtor** determines the impression the customers would have about you and whatever you're selling. For example, if you're going to be making a video of yourself inviting people to your open house, your video should be short, precise, and filled with only relevant information. A long and boring video with a lot of unnecessary talk would have people sleeping while your video plays, and we're sure that's not the reaction you desire.

Also, for the photos of the house or short video clips, it'll be better to get professionals to make the videos or take the pictures for a more alluring look. We're pretty sure no one would love to come to an open house where the sampled pictures of the house look all blurry and ugly. The fonts of the texts on your fliers and business cards should have an appropriate size and the entire piece of the right coloring to ensure it's not looking all tacky.

3.Prepare the Home for Open House Tours

The next thing to do would be to get the apartment ready for the tour. You should ensure the **house is decluttered**. The guests shouldn't come in and find shoes, books, or other stuff lying around because it'll make the place look less appealing. The place should be thoroughly cleaned and inspected to know if any repairs should be made, like a leaking roof or a spoilt tap. The house should be repainted both inside and outside, with the lawns mowed to put the house in perfect condition.

There's a current imbalance in supply and demand for homes since properties are spending fewer days on the market. We're living in a seller's market, meaning there are more buyers than property listings of houses for sale. Even in these situations, it would be detrimental to host an open house before **preparing the property** for it.

Potential homebuyers pay special attention to property details. If there are major flaws, don't expect the buyers to ignore those issues. They'll either opt out or make a lower offer than the home's market value based on those flaws.

Talk to the property owner and ensure the **home is ready for an open house**. Some essential ways to help you prepare the home include:

- Mowing the lawn
- Fixing broken doors and windows
- Repainting the front door
- Cleaning and decluttering

Another important step in preparing the home for an open house is **depersonalization**. You don't want to give potential homebuyers an idea that there's a family currently living there. The key is to allow the buyers to picture themselves living in that space. You can't achieve this with family pictures on the walls. Hire a professional house stager to make the home more attractive by highlighting its strengths.

Rope in the Neighbors

People aren't just buying the property. They're investing in the neighborhood as well. You can inform your neighbors about the open house, encourage them to pass by, view the house, and mingle with the rest of the community. You can encourage them to ask any questions pertaining to the property itself, its value, or general real estate queries.

Most neighbors want to peep into the property. It's human nature and it isn't a crime to want to do so. They would love an invite to come and take a look without feeling like they're engaging in illegal activity.

However, why should you invite them when they already have their own homes?

Because **they may know someone who's looking for exactly what you're selling**. Remember, word of mouth in real estate is really important. It's much easier to sell the house to someone who's familiar with the neighborhood instead of a stranger.

4. Marketing

Since you want people to attend the open house, you must let them know about it. Top performing realtors maximize their networks to **spread the word** and have several people attend the open house.

We understand that not all realtors are well-connected, especially newbies. Luckily, there are a few other marketing strategies you can use to achieve this goal. If you're an old-school guy, you can put up a large sign in front of the property and around places with traffic in the neighborhood. You can also pay for an advertisement slot in your local newspapers and magazines.

In this digital age, you can't ignore the power of social media. Use your social media accounts to promote the open house on Facebook, Twitter, and Instagram. Don't forget to post on realtor groups and other real estate pages. If you can, hire a professional videographer to make high-quality videos for TikTok and Instagram reels.

Other online platforms you can consider include **Craigslist and real estate listing sites**, such as MLS, Zillow, realtor.com, and Trulia. Don't forget to include the open house date on whatever platform you choose.

Here are some more ideas you can follow to spread the word:

Previewing Previous Video Montage

It is critical to publish content on your real estate website on a regular basis. No, this does not mean you have to spend half your day staring at a computer screen.

It does, however, imply that you should spend your time intelligently developing material that will strike the perfect chord with the suitable demographic – something that is simple to achieve with effective real estate video marketing.

Put together all the materials you have for the open house and listing. Some of these materials should include video and audio recordings of you speaking with customers, snacks, drinks or refreshments you share, property tour film, pictures of the exterior of listings, and much more.

Create a more extended version of this to use as one of your critical branding assets to promote on your homepage and elsewhere on your website. Promote all of your open houses and show what it's like to visit your listings as a salesman.

Share these videos on your social media platforms! It could be Instagram, Facebook, or Twitter; just ensure you use the internet to spread the word.

Instagram Geo-tagging

This is a no-brainer for realtors as your companies are location-based. Simply tagging a specific geographic area in your Instagram post or story is an Instagram geotag. On Instagram when looking for a geotag, we can see the posts that other users have made with that particular tag.

Your post can live in the geotagged place if you add a geotag to it. Your post can turn up when other Instagram users look for the same geotag or click on it in another image. For this reason, Instagram posts with a geotag get 79% higher engagement than those without one.

Simply geotag your posts to draw in users looking for homes nearby and increase the number of people who will see your listings. Use your city and any noteworthy neighborhoods or districts as tags.

Active searchers are more likely to be further along in the purchasing process, making it simpler to turn them into leads.

Multiple listing services (MLS)

As a realtor, you benefit significantly from gaining access to the MLS site. In addition to enhancing the public visibility of your property, the platform is exclusively limited to licensed agents, so the inquiries and offers you get will be from more highly qualified clients.

That saves you a ton of time and energy when it comes to showings and open house events.

Every time you have an open house, you have to hurry to have everything arranged and gleaming clean, then you have to flee until the prospective buyers have spent as much time as they need to check every element of your property with a fine-toothed comb.

When your first pool of prospects is screened by the MLS, you will likely perform fewer showings before receiving a good offer.

Social media ADs

This is yet another crucial marketing strategy that will increase your visibility. There are currently 4.5 billion social media users around the world. This means that posting your event on social media has the potential to reach millions of people.

You can publicize your event by publishing your event flier or preferred videos on your own Facebook account, your business page if you have one, real estate groups, and your narrative. Consider running a paid advertisement to reach a larger audience. This one allows you to send your material to the people who suit your chosen demographic.

You can utilize these platforms to reach your target audience.

You should also explore other options like posting on your social media platform i.e. Instagram handles and stories, Twitter, Pinterest, and LinkedIn.

Influencer Marketing

In the real estate industry, a lot is changing. According to one study, approximately 90% of business owners believe that influencer marketing tactics are effective.

You can pay an influencer to promote your product or service. The influencer would promote you and encourage their followers to follow your pages using this strategy. On their page, the influencer would also regularly repost your fliers, images of your property, and videos. They could also organize giveaway sections to their enormous following to entice more people to pay attention to you, and most importantly, they could claim they'll be there at the event, and bam, all their favorite admirers would want to come.

You simply need to find the right influencer whose active followers correspond to your target market, and you're good to go. You'd be surprised how quickly your event will become a social media trend, how your brand as a whole will gain visibility even for future events, and how it will translate to a massive turnout at your open house.

Email Advertising

Given that, 91% of customers check their email on a regular basis and 77% prefer permission-based marketing via email, emailing listings and open houses to leads will deliver a higher return on investment than other marketing channels.

You should email folks on your database at least one week before the event with the videos you've already created, plus another short reminder message two days before the event. We believe you should have an email list if you haven't already.

Include inviting presentations in your emails, spice it up with some storytelling, and be selective about when you send them.

After working hours, when people can go through their less official emails is a good time.

Door-to-door invitation

We understand that knocking on the door of someone you've never met can be awkward, but there is no better way to get known in your community than to get out there and meet people face to face.

We suggest you visit dozens of homes in the neighborhood and distribute information about your upcoming event. Many of them would be uncomfortable with it, but that's fine; what matters is the brand awareness you're creating.

There's no need to rush; instead, be subtle and persuasive. Make sure to leave a flier advertising your open house and contact information.

If you have neighbors with whom you are already acquainted, you can invite them over for tea or a drink before the main event and give them tiny teasers to make them interested and invite their friends.

It is not a high-pressure sales pitch; please keep this in mind. Ultimately, leave the decision in your neighbor's hands, but show enthusiasm and willingness.

Create Signage

Open house signs signify that a house or property is available for public viewing.

When a realtor sells a home, he or she may put up many open house signs. Sometimes people put up signs away from the house, perhaps a block or two away or on the main cross street, with big letters announcing an open house and an arrow pointing in the right direction. Arrows should point in the appropriate direction to avoid confusing potential purchasers. Depending on where you are, the method for attaching each sign may differ.

Another type of open house sign is typically put immediately in front of the house. It should be large enough so that passers-by can read it.

People should consider their intentions when choosing an open house sign or a set of them. They are attempting to sell a house or other property. In this regard, foot traffic is beneficial because more visitors may indicate more possible purchasers, yet the signage may occasionally draw someone who is only interested in observing and not bidding. It is, therefore, critical to make the sign visible and easy to read because signs that are ignored will not sell a home.

Partner With Other Professionals

One of the most surprising lessons in your real estate career is finding out that you should **view other real estate agents as collaborators**, instead of competitors. If you've noticed a listing for sale in the same neighborhood, you can reach out to the listing agent, plan a collaborative open house, promote it, and host together.

The best thing about this strategy is that you can combine the numbers and tap into a larger pool of potential buyers. You can leverage both your networks, pool resources for marketing, and spread the staging fees to make it more affordable for you. Besides, neighbors become curious when there's more than one open house in their neighborhood.

It would also be helpful to work with a lender or loan officer and have them present during the open house to answer any financing questions from potential buyers on the spot. The loan officer can provide pre-qualifications, payments, and interest rates on-site, which can fast-track the lending process and save you and the buyer time.

If you're showcasing a large house, **you can build a team** so that you can have someone present on each floor to answer questions and discuss the property's talking points. If it's an apartment, have someone in the lobby to welcome the visitors and usher them upstairs where you'll be waiting for them.

Don't forget to share the key talking points with every professional on your team so that the message stays consistent.

As you can see, hosting an open house doesn't have to be stressful. Initially, it might seem like a huge task, but you will get used to it with time. Hosting a successful open house regularly can be the key to building a consistent flow of clients for your real estate business.

Remember, the more people you reach, the more you increase your buyer pool. Hosting an open house the first weekend a house is on sale generates a number of interested buyers. Don't forget to implement these marketing strategies a week or so before the open house.

5. Go to the house earlier

After all, the preparation has been done and the D-Day comes, you should go to the house an hour earlier than the appointed time for the open house. This is so you'd do some finishing touches like opening the windows to showcase natural lighting, setting up your music equipment (You'll be needing it to create a soothing atmosphere), putting your feedback sheets at the strategic locations, putting your scented candles and a whole lot of other things that'll make the guests feel relaxed.

The exterior design on that day should also be eye-catching such that one who is casually driving by might decide to stop for a second to see what's going on. An important aspect of hosting an open house is the **ability to give your guests an incredible experience**; that's why it won't be bad to share some food, wine, or snacks. When the guests are made to feel at home, they tend to be more comfortable talking to you on a personal level.

You could also decorate the house with some eye-catching pieces of art. These types of things are the perfect conversation starters. A guest could be like, "wow, this is a beautiful work of art, where did you get it from?"And from answering the question, you could go ahead and talk about other things. You'll also want to dress smartly and appropriately because all the little things are what people would rate your pricing with.

6. D-Day

When all is set, and the guests start coming in, you have to be very polite to them, use appropriate language and tone, and be very careful not to follow them around too much, so they don't feel any pressure. After welcoming them, you can tell them to **collect the feedback papers** and fill them in because you'd like to know how they feel. You can put in questions like:

- What did you like most about the property?
- Do you think the pricing of the house is fair?
- How did you hear about this open house?
- Do you find the sizes of the rooms big enough?

There could also be boxes to tick that'll show if they're currently house hunting, planning on buying a house sometime later, or just looking around. Most importantly, the feedback sheet should have a space for the guest's contact information. This is important because that's how you're going to get your leads. You can also hand in your business card to some guests, telling them how they can always reach out to you if they have any questions or help.

7. Follow-up

Finally, when everyone is gone and you're done basking in the euphoria of your successful event, it'll be time for more work. Having plenty of guests would end up as just guests and not prospective clients without the right follow-up. You must have had quite a large number of people who dropped their contact information, and what you should do is follow them up. You'd start by **sending emails thanking them** for gracing your event. From the feedback papers, you should know who to concentrate on. For those who mentioned specific things they were looking out for that they didn't see, you can suggest other houses that match their description. For those who liked the house, you can suggest you fix a meeting.

Hosting one open house right might be the route to that big break you've been looking for in your real estate business because if you follow the tips above, you're sure going to have lots of guests in your open house who are most likely going to become potential clients.

CHAPTER SIX

LISTING PRESENTATION

It is quite challenging to obtain a listing since it is clear that the most outstanding realtors in the market continue to receive practically all of the business, leaving the less well-known realtors in the background. Because of the inability to win listings, a staggering **87% of realtors quit the industry**.

However, being among the top realtors who bag the most listings and stay in business is definitely attainable with adequate preparation for your listing appointment and presentation. In this article, we'll be walking you through the 8 steps to prepare for your listing appointment and presentation.

1. Know the Property

Knowing the house you're attempting to list is crucial for someone who has just been issued a listing appointment. This will give you the knowledge you need to continue putting together the other materials required for the appointment.

You should be aware of specifics, such as the number of bedrooms, the sort of house it is—whether it's an apartment, a single-family home, or something else—as well as **its positive and negative attributes**.

Additional inquiries, such as whether the house has recently been renovated or whether there are any outstanding liens on the property, should be determined.

2. Know the Seller

You should do your homework on potential clients just like someone seeking a job would do their homework on the company for which they are being interviewed. Before the appointment, conduct a Google, Facebook, Instagram, or LinkedIn search to learn more about the **interests or backgrounds of your possible clients**.

You should also be aware of the client's expectations from a listing agent, as well as how driven they are to sell their home, why they want to sell, how fast they need it sold, and the price for which they plan to sell the property. Look into your client's marital status, whether they have children, are single, or both, where they want to relocate, and any other pertinent information.

With this knowledge, you'll be able to determine what material is relevant to the client's interests and what you should include in your listing presentation during your visit.

3. Conduct a Neighborhood Research

After you've obtained as much information as possible about the subject property and potential sellers, you should gather as much information as possible about the neighborhood in which the house is located.

To properly prepare for your visit and presentation, you must have a thorough **awareness of the community and market** around the seller's home.

You should have answers to questions like how many properties have sold in the area lately? What ranking systems exist for schools? How low or high is the crime rate? What are the best restaurants? Is the neighborhood affected by traffic congestion or other nuisances that might affect the property before you go for your listing appointment and presentation?

4. Comparative Market Analysis

A comparative market study is a strategy used by real estate agents to determine the worth of a given property by comparing it to previously sold comparable properties in the area.

The research considers the location, size, structure, style, age, and other attributes of the property, as well as that of comparables, to establish the price.

Conduct this **comparative market research** to assess the property's worth using the information you've gathered about the area and the house you're hoping the client will list with you.

It is wise to prepare this analysis beforehand because it will be included in the presentation to your client. To make this analysis, you should visit your Multiple Listing Service and contrast the property with recently sold listings that are comparable. This will demonstrate your professionalism as a realtor and your local expertise.

Additionally, it serves as a reality check for sellers whose expectations regarding the asking price of their home may be exaggerated.

5. Preview Available listings

There is no denying that the photographs supplied by the Multiple Listing Service do not always adequately reflect the house. To do a more thorough analysis, **you must physically inspect the homes after visiting your MLS** for your comparative analysis.

This allows you to know the precise specifics of the house as it is because your presentation will suffer significantly from ignorance of such facts.

Visiting other homes beforehand gives you greater assurance in your presentation, and better presentations come from more assured speakers, which translates into local competency in the eyes of your potential clients.

6. Send Pre-listing Information Packet

A pre-listing packet aims to enlighten potential clients about the selling process and persuade them to deal with you. This packet is provided to your prospect before the real listing consultation to give them some background about you, demonstrate how you work, and highlight the benefits they can expect.

It contains a booklet introducing your agency or real estate company, your promise or warranty, prior performance statistics, past client testimonials, and sales procedure data. It also includes the questions most clients tend to ask during the actual listing presentation appointment with the answers.

Pre-listing presentations demonstrate your commitment to provide exceptional customer service while significantly reducing the time spent on explanations on the day of the listing appointment and increasing the time available for questions or interviews.

A strong **pre-listing presentation can be an effective tool** in your marketing toolbox, and make you stand out from your rivals. On the other hand, a weak pre-listing presentation or none at all may reduce your chances of landing a listing and make the actual listing appointment more difficult than it should have been.

The Pre-listing information packet should be delivered three days before the actual appointment day, so the client can take time to study it and give you the necessary feedback on the listing appointment day.

7. Aesthetically Pleasing Listing Presentation

Real estate agents who plan their listing presentation script ahead of time might convert more in-person meetings with potential clients into actual clients.

Face-to-face interactions can be nerve-racking for certain real estate professionals, and they may tend to forget important items they should mention during the presentation. However, by **writing your presentation script in advance** of the meeting, you would be preventing that from happening.

The presentation should comprise your résumé, accomplishments, the number of homes you've sold in the past, client testimonials, a description of the sales method, the strategies you'll employ to sell the house, and the pricing, along with an explanation of how you determined the price.

As a tool to facilitate seamless selling, the customer's obligations, such as decluttering, cleaning up after renovations, and staging, should be incorporated into the presentation.

Preparing all this information in advance is undoubtedly beneficial; we cannot overlook the significance of a tidy presentation layout with gorgeous images and graphs. A well-organized presentation **simplifies the entire presentation process and makes you appear more professional.**

You must, however, be sure to keep your cool and project confidence during the presentation. To accomplish this, practice the presentation pitch aloud to reduce anxiety before meeting the home seller.

8. Rehearse Your Listing Presentation

It is typical to feel anxious before presentations. You must, however, be sure to keep your cool and project confidence during the presentation.

To accomplish this, **practice the presentation pitch thoroughly** before meeting with the home seller to help reduce anxiety. The presentation should be repeatedly practiced until you feel confident in delivering it.

If you can grasp the main concepts of your presentation, you will be better able to manage your anxiety, and you will be able to enter the room with assurance and concentrate on what truly matters which is developing a close relationship with the home sellers, outlining all the facts, and ultimately winning them as clients.

CHAPTER SEVEN

FOLLOW-UP

As a realtor, you must have noticed that not all your prospects convert to clients, In fact, perhaps only be one or two out of 100 prospects end up becoming clients!

Does it make you feel like you're doing so much but having so few results? Do you give up on those prospects that don't buy and focus on getting new leads?

You're leaving a lot of money on the table! One reason why you might be experiencing this is that you don't follow-up with those prospects. As soon as they don't buy, you take it that the deal is over and give up too easily.

Here's good news for you; even if your prospects don't need you right now, it doesn't mean they won't need you in the future, and staying in touch with them will keep you at the top of their minds.

With the right follow-up systems and strategies, you'll be able to turn more prospects into clients, even if they have rejected your offer twice or thrice before! These follow-up strategies and scripts will help increase your lead conversion rate and increase your business in no time at all.

How To Follow-up With Your Leads

Emails

One of the best ways to follow-up with real estate leads is through emails. It's an increasingly preferred and nearly always appropriate communication method. Why? Because through emails, you can regularly stay at the top of your prospect's mind.

Follow-up emails are essential to maintain relationships with prospects and clients alike as they increase your chances of closing a sale.

If you're wanting to connect with buyers who have a longer time frame, sending a follow-up email is exactly what you need to do, and with a drip campaign, things can get even easier.

As a realtor, you could receive additional leads that may not be ready to immediately buy or sell, but with follow-up emails, you can nurture them and help move them closer to a transaction.

In clearer terms, here are a few reasons why you should always send follow-up emails:

- Buyers generally prefer emails as they get to read them in their leisure time.
- They're excellent for long-term leads. According to survey data from Zillow Group Consumer Housing Trends Report in 2019, buyers usually spend an average of about 4.5 months shopping for a new home to buy. On the other hand, sellers spend up to six months on average just thinking about listing their home, and those who have owned their home longer take even more time to decide if they're to sell.

- As a real estate agent, it gives you an opportunity for personalization as you can reference your prospects' answers in your follow-up emails and build rapport with them.
- Follow-up Emails drive business; you can encourage the buyer to connect over the phone, book an appointment, and then eventually complete a sale.

While writing follow-up Emails, there are a few things you should note:

- Be quick to get to the point. Most prospects will likely skim through at first. It should be worth it.
- Keep your follow-up emails short. Only include two to three clarifying questions at a time.
- Make it personable by using the prospect's name while greeting and thanking them for their time.
- Help your prospects understand why you need a response by detailing your next steps. Give them a reason to connect with you by telling them when you'll be available next or how you can help them.
- Include a call to action that is easy to respond to. Include your phone number so they can call or text you.
- Don't send emails too frequently or try to hard sell your prospects. It'll only annoy your prospects.

Want to benefit from our highly effective done-for-you follow-up email sequences? go to https://soldouthouses.com/followup for more info.

Phone Calls:

If you ask any buyer or seller, they'll likely tell you that the 'follow-up caller' is one of their least favorite persons, and it's not so hard to tell why.

Unlike emails, phone calls are much more intrusive, and a lot of people become annoyed. That's why most Realtors set reminders and end up staring at their notes and trying to come up with excuses as to why they won't call their prospects, like "They're probably busy! Or I don't want to bother them!" Does this sound familiar?

Well, you don't have to. You don't also have to ignore the classic follow-up phone calls, which have worked the trick for several real estate agents like you for many years. The only thing here is that you have to make sure you're doing it correctly or else you may wish you hadn't called.

One way to ensure you'll get the desired results through follow-up phone calls is to be prepared. Having a script for different scenarios will help you achieve that. Instead of ending up clueless for lack of words to say, a script that you can loosely follow will help you stay on track so that you won't get lost in the conversation. That way, you can confidently follow-up your leads with phone calls which can be crucial to your business. Here's how...

A few very important reasons you need to utilize phone calls for your follow-up is that it helps you personalize your interactions with prospects. With phone calls, you have the chance to introduce yourself, ask questions, and directly answer the questions your prospects have as they're asked, address the objections of your prospects in real-time, immediately countering their arguments if need be, and also forging a stronger connection with buyers and sellers alike. That's something, isn't it?

You might ask. "When is the best time to call a lead?" Well, from research, any time between 4 pm and 5 pm is the best time to pick up the phone; 8 am and 10 am happens to be the next best time. However, regardless of when you want to call, never attempt to follow-up through phone calls on the weekends. Don't do it.

Follow-up calls aim to build rapport with prospects and not to hard-sell them. Build rapport, and the opportunity to sell to them or book an appointment will come.

Sometimes, you won't be able to reach your prospect on the first try. That's okay. What's not okay is to hang up and call it a day. Instead, leave a voicemail revealing your identity and reason for calling. It'll either get them to call back or give you a better chance the next time you'd decide to call them. Win-win!

Text Messages:

Granted, calls can be scary and quite challenging, especially if you're unprepared or just shy. That doesn't mean you can't follow-up with your prospects. Whether you're comfortable with calls or not, you can use the option of sending a text message instead of, or in addition to, a phone call or voicemail.

In many cases, texts prove more effective than phone calls because some people hate talking on the phone, but they're usually happy to text or read their texts.

It may surprise you to know that the vast majority of people actually want you to text them; a National Association of Realtors report found that up to 62% of all home buyers prefer their agent to send property information through text messages.

Text messages have an open rate of 98%, and this helps realtors to stay in front of clients, improve response rates, generate more leads, quickly find buyers, stay in touch with prospects, and keep them updated on open houses, new listings, and any other relevant information.

Getting amazing results when following up with prospects with text messages entails being strategic. A few steps are needed to get the job done.

The first step is to ensure you have the right contact information and reach out to prospects at the right time. You must also have a good reason for contacting them.

You ought to get a response from your contacts when you reach out. To achieve this, your text needs to be personal and relevant. Be sure to address your prospects by name. It gets their attention and makes them more apt to respond.

As soon as they take action, reach out to them. If they've just visited your website, send them a 'Thank you" message for their interest.

Note: Don't reply immediately, even if you're using an automated system. When you do that, it makes them think it's an autoresponder and puts them off. Make it look natural. Wait a few minutes. It'll do the trick.

Keep your messages short and straight to the point. Ask a question or make one request at a time.

Ensure that you have a good reason for reaching out. Ask for feedback on your service. Offer a free consultation. Whatever the reason, be sure that it's clear in your message.

Don't send promotions or unsolicited messages to your leads. It will just annoy them, and they'll likely unsubscribe from your list.

Always include your contact information in every follow-up text message you send so the contact can reach you if they have any questions.

With these tips, you'll surely write follow-up text messages that get the desired responses.

Retargeting:

Retargeting is a very sophisticated way to follow-up with prospects. It helps you reach out to leads that have previously visited your website.

A retargeting tool like Facebook pixel can aid in tracking your prospects after they have left your website. With these tools, there's no escape for the prospect because even when they go to other unrelated websites, they'll still see your ads. Sweet, right?

With those ads, they'll be reminded about their real estate problem and that your service can help them solve it. Win-win!

Retargeted leads are more likely to click on your ad because they're already "warmed up."

After setting up the ad and routing leads back to your website, you will have successfully followed-up, but there's a catch. You might be tempted to think you've done it all, but you haven't. Instead of sending prospects back to your home page, send them to an optimized lead magnet instead so they can sign up to your email list to get the freebie.

Now, you can build a relationship with them and eventually get them to be your client!

Social Media:

With so many leads on social media, it's disastrous not take advantage.

Several leads, buyers, and sellers alike can contact you by engaging with your posts. Some might even indicate interest in your services through social media, and it's up to you to make them go over the line and follow through with a deal.

That's why you need to take your follow-up on social media very seriously. Whether on Facebook, Twitter, or Instagram, you can reach out to leads who have shown an interest and build rapport with them in the DMs.

By doing that, you can answer some of the questions they have and schedule an appointment or a call or even recommend a free resource that can help them, which will make them leave their contact details in the process for further communication.

It's not the popular follow-up system for Realtors, but it's certainly worth considering because it's quite as effective as the others. You should try it.

Face-to-face Follow-up

When it comes to following up with prospects, most real estate agents tend to look past this method but should they? Definitely not!

Face-to-face visits are one of the best approaches when done right, as it puts you in personal communication with the prospect. However, it must be done with the permission of the prospect.

You can achieve this by booking an appointment via a text message, a phone call, or an email. When the prospect consents to it, a date and time should be arranged, and then you can proceed.

It's particularly useful to Realtors who have just a few prospects each month as they'll have the time needed. With this method, you'll have a higher chance of converting more, even with fewer prospects.

This is because face-to-face follow-up conversations, being the most personal, allows for more direct interaction and will help you read the prospect's nonverbal signals and body reactions, which are very helpful.

CHAPTER EIGHT

NEGOTIATION AND CLOSING THE DEAL

This is where the money comes into play. Now that you have done all the work, you have a hungry person in front of you and they want what you are offering, it is time to construct and give them the deal they can't say no to. In selling, the deal or the offer is everything. If you don't have the right deal or the right offer in place, nothing else matters. To ensure that you have the right offer at the right time, here are some tips and tricks that will help you close the deal.

Understand the other party's needs

Rushing into a negotiation without getting to know the other side will put you at a great disadvantage. Any real estate transaction will be won by the party with the most information since the more you **know about the seller or buyer**, the better you will be able to comprehend their purpose and utilize it to your advantage.

If you learn, for instance, that the buyer adores luxury, you may continue to cite the opulent features of your home as the justification for your pricing. This would appeal to them as it is what they are interested in, and they would, in turn, be willing to pay a larger sum to acquire the property.

Additionally, if you are the buyer's realtor, understanding the **seller's motivation and needs** will assist you in negotiating successfully on your client's behalf.

For instance, if the seller is in trouble and has to sell the property quickly, this would indicate that the seller's main concern is not price but rather timing, and as a result, you can appeal to the seller's need by reiterating how capable you are to acquire the house as quickly as possible.

Avoid showing desperation

Being desperate is a bad technique, and you don't have to be an expert in real estate negotiation to understand that. Making important decisions when you're feeling emotional is never a good idea, and this is especially true when you're negotiating real estate contracts.

As a selling agent, it is advisable to **avoid displaying how eager you are to sell a property** because the opposing party can use it as a rationale to underprice the home.

You should set a limit and control your emotions no matter how much you love the property to prevent getting misled into paying more than you bargained for.

Make them think saying yes is their idea

A successful negotiation requires making the person on the other side of the table feel at ease at all times. This is done by having them believe that agreeing to the terms was their idea.

No one likes to feel forced into doing something; therefore, competent negotiators frequently **employ subtle engagement strategies** to give the other side the impression that they are in charge. It has been proven that reminding them constantly that they are free to decline your request is one effective technique to accomplish this.

According to studies, this tactic has a high compliance rate since it makes the other side feel less compelled to accept the offer.

Putting your attention on generating value and meeting needs is another approach to accomplish this. **Negotiations should not be a do-or-die situation**; instead, you should take the time to be receptive to needs, establish rapport, and foster trust.

Focus on the emotions involved

During a negotiation, a good realtor should be proficient at leveraging people's emotions since both monetary and emotional considerations affect property sales.

If a potential buyer displayed a keen interest in the property or displayed any signs of desperation, the seller would likely **offer a higher price** for it. As a listing agent, you can take advantage of this information during your negotiation.

Also, if you are the buyer's agent, you should continually be on the lookout for the seller's emotive points and utilize them as leverage during the negotiation.

The most crucial factor to consider is if everyone involved is satisfied with the deal and received what they wanted; therefore, you should always **communicate with everyone and appeal to their emotions.**

Create a win-win situation

The best negotiators are those who develop scenarios in which both parties end up winning. A win-win negotiation is a kind of negotiation strategy that focuses on **achieving the best result for all parties** participating in the process.

A substantial degree of understanding, compromise, and teamwork is a cornerstone to a successful negotiation as you plan how to create a win-win situation.

This strategy is particularly successful since it makes the parties frequently consider not only their interests but also those of the opposing party, providing some degree of fairness in the agreement.

By downplaying your benefits and highlighting the advantages of the opposing side, the win-win bargaining method often results in an **agreement that is satisfactory to both parties.**

However, to avoid overcompensating or leaving an agreement unfulfilled after satisfying the other party's demands, it is essential to identify the parts of the contract where you are willing to make concessions even before the negotiations begin.

Put an expiration date on any counter-offers

After you establish your listing price, multiple offers will typically come in that are less than that price, and as a result, negotiations will take place that involves **sending counter offers** to the other party. As a realtor acting as the seller's agent, you should inform the buyer that your client is looking to close as soon as possible.

Some buyers and their agents often waste a lot of time getting back to the other party regarding their counter offers during negotiations, which can be a setback. When a counteroffer is outstanding, a seller's home is temporarily off the market, preventing them from receiving additional offers.

If the deal eventually fails, your house will spend more time on the market, and the more days your home is on the market, the less desirable it appears, making it less likely to get a buyer who would buy it at a reasonable price.

When the buyer or agent makes an offer, which you respond to using a counteroffer, you should **place a deadline on that counteroffer**. It would indicate that you have other options available that you look forward to utilizing, and that would encourage them to move the process along quickly if they don't want to lose the house to another individual

Be on top of your bidding war game

In real estate, a bidding war can happen when more than one potential buyer is making an offer on a home. These buyers compete to become the new owner of the property by incrementally increasing their offers, often pushing the price higher than the original property value.

Inciting a **bidding war is a bargaining strategy** that'll help you net more money than the market value of your home. To create these bidding wars, realtors can disclose that there are other bids so that it can result in higher offers.

The seller is legally allowed to counter more than one offer simultaneously, but they must include appropriate language letting all the parties know of the situation.

Another strategy that can assist in starting a bidding battle is purposefully **offering your house for less than its fair market value**. Reduced prices would most likely spur higher interest in a property and rivalry among purchasers.

However, there are risks involved, so it's crucial to avoid going too low because you don't want to market your house for much less than you're willing to accept.

Be willing to walk away

Learning to say no and knowing when to leave a negotiation is one of the trickiest strategies to master. Although knowing when to walk away can be challenging, it all comes down to knowing your client and what he or she is or is not prepared to give up.

Before the negotiation, you should know your client's maximum purchasing price or lowest selling price, as the case may be. If you and the opposing party aren't close to the same ballpark early on, then it's **best to walk away and work with someone else** rather than wasting time negotiating and renegotiating.

This strategy, if used by the seller's realtor, communicates your confidence in the value of the property and your asking price while also saving you time because when you outrightly reject an offer, you can proceed to enter other negotiations and accept higher offers.

The easiest way to deal with lowballers who have come to engage in back and forth is to utilize this method because if you give them counteroffers, you might be delaying the sale of your house.

However, if you outrightly reject the offer, they'll know that **someone may make a better offer** at any moment and would be pressured into re-submitting reasonable offers quickly if they're interested in the property.

Always have a plan B

It is very unlikely that you will be able to strike the exact deal that you or your client desire unless the market is significantly in your favor; therefore, you have to be ready for the worst scenario and the best way to be prepared for that is **by having a plan B**.

It is crucial for a realtor to always have a backup plan in place because it will help you decide when to back out or sign a contract. Having a backup plan reduces anxiety and puts your mind at ease, enabling you to maintain composure and control your emotions throughout the negotiation process.

It also informs your decision because if you have a backup plan, you'll be less likely to accept unattractive deals knowing that you have alternative options to consider. However, without a backup strategy, you can **end up making a concession** that would work against you.

To have an effective plan B, you must understand what your client is and is not prepared to give up. Additionally, you must ascertain the fundamental principles and values of the opposing negotiator. If this information is discovered from the beginning of the negotiation process, there will be much less back and forth.

Last-Minute Closing

It often happens that all the aspects of our sales process have been well sorted out professionally only for the client to lose interest at the last minute. You have done so much work to come this far and the client is actually satisfied with the listing appointment. However, most clients will still try to negotiate for a slight reduction in price at the last minute. This moment is the exact moment a smart realtor should never miss as it is a perfect time to close the deal perfectly.

How do you do this?

It is simple. Simply just agree to the price reduction and immediately ask them if they are willing to sign the deal today or right now. You can also push further by offering to prepare all the necessary documents right away before the seller changes his or her mind. This way, your client will rightly feel you have his or her interest in mind and he or she will likely agree to bring the deal to a close as soon as possible.

This works like magic and I am certain you will be grateful you tried it. The reason it works is also clear. Your client is already in love with your services and he or she is only looking for last-minute benefits. Most realtors will say no or delay their response until everything becomes cold again. You have not given your client any excuse and they will most likely have **no choice but to say yes** to your request!

The Yes or Yes Closing Technique

Only smart realtors know this secret I am about to tell you in this article. We all know that everyone likes to feel in control of the situation they are in. The same goes for clients. The moment a client feels that he or she is no longer in control of a situation, they lose interest in the transaction. Your sole duty is to make your client feel at ease and you have to be smart about it.

There are several roads to a destination as there are several ways to acquire a top-notch property. Give your client **multiple options that lead to a result**. No one likes one option as it makes it seem as if they have no choice. Clearly tell them the pros of choosing a particular property over another and the cons of every option in the list. However, you must try to make sure that the cons do not significantly outweigh the pros.

I am not saying you should be dishonest. We have emphasized honesty on this channel many times as it is the topmost quality of a smart realtor. If you discover that the cons of a property are greater than the pros, that property is not for the client and you should not include it in the options.

The Act Fast Closing Technique

This is probably the most popular technique on our list. This method works by creating a sense of urgency. You want the client to know how important it is for him to close the deal now. It works mostly for sellers but can also work for buyers.

How do you go about it?

The first thing is to do an intensive study of the property and note all the reasons why it is the right moment to sell this property now or buy the property now! There are high chances that you will find some reasons. Tell your client all these reasons you have noted and professionally advise him or her that it is the **perfect time to sell or purchase** this property at the perfect price.

This technique is a blockbuster! It works best when one party is ready to sign the deal but the other is reluctant. If your reasons are genuine, the reluctant one will most likely have no choice but to succumb to the deal.

Taking A Walk Closing Technique

This is another technique that works best for sellers. It is a technique that makes your client feel that you understand their property well and he or she becomes confident that he will get his property sold at the best price possible. Take a walk with your client around the property and inside the property. He knows his property, but you are the professional realtor. You see what your client doesn't see, and you know the most valuable parts of the property.

As you take the walk with your clients, highlight the valuable aspects of the property and why you think people might be interested in it. You can say something like 'this bedroom is small, but it is well suited to be a mini-library for those who would like to have privacy while reading'. Your client sees this as a weakness in the property, but you have made him realize it might be a strength after all. How else do you gain someone's trust so easily?!

This technique works because the **client becomes confident** that his or her property is in the hands of a hardworking expert and he or she becomes easily committed to the process of selling. He or she will sign the deal in no time and you both win.

Clearing Your Doubts Closing Technique

Some clients might seem very confusing to realtors. You have done everything you can to convince him or her to sell the property, but you are not certain if your client is convinced yet. This technique works best if the client hesitates even when the other party is ready. Don't be frustrated. Just an inquiry will solve it all!

Be specific in the questions you ask your client. Ask your client **if he or she has an issue with his or her current property** and why he or she thinks a new property will be better than the current property. This way, you will know if your client is convinced to sell the property or not.

If you feel there is a valid reason to sell the property, assure your client that you are about to sell it for him or her at the best possible price and you are ready to find them their dream property.

Make Me Special Closing Technique

This is not a common technique used by realtors, but it might just be the magic you have been looking for. It is important to make your client feel that **you have his or her interest at heart** from the beginning of any transaction. It is understandable that we might be sometimes overwhelmed by our desire to make money that we forget to do this.

Organize a special meeting with your client and give him or her all the information you can. Summarize all the details of the transaction so far and highlight how you think the property will satisfy his or her desires and boost his or her status. You can even offer bonuses as most clients also like to get the most out of a transaction.

Relax!

Yes! You heard it right! Sometimes all these techniques discussed today might not work out. Do not be disturbed. It is just the perfect time to relax. Sleep it off and **give the client ample time to make his or her decisions**. Some clients might just be afraid to sign the deal while others are just unsure. Give them time to ease the pressure and that might just be the key that will open the lock!

Now you can be confident of closing sales just at the perfect time with one of these techniques discussed. The techniques can also be combined to achieve perfection.

There you go.

You have closed your deal; your money is sitting comfortably in your bank and life is good. Well, not really. You need to get up again tomorrow and do it all over again. This is the life of the realtor. It is a life filled with deals, opportunities and a good life for those that can really sink their teeth into the process and make it their own.

In all reality, you are your own boss. You are selling a specific product that fills a specific need. The more you learn and the better you get at it, the greater the success you will have.

THE MILLIONAIRE REAL ESTATE AGENT BY GARY KELLER BOOK SUMMARY

This book will teach you, Why you need to have more sales. The relationship between being a real estate agent and the moon landing. Why do you need to have passive income? There are many helpful things that you can learn from this book. So let's dive into "The Millionaire Real Estate Agent" book summary to learn some critical lessons about the real estate business.

Lesson 1: To become a better real estate agent you need to understand the reasoning behind motivation

Whenever someone gets a big work item or big project, the first instinct is to dive in and start working. And with this approach people underestimate the **power of planning**. It might work in the short term; however, to work in the long term, you need to understand the reason to do it before doing anything else.

In the chapter *"Think a Million"*, we learn how all the high performer's function. They define their purpose and motivation, and this helps them stay focused. You can witness this same power of purpose and motivation too. When you have a clear goal in mind, you feel even more motivated to plan and execute. Of course, it gets difficult to find motivation every single day, and that is why it is important to find something that gives you a constant sense of purpose.

One particularly important thing to remember is that when we think about **purpose and motivation**, having an internal motivation to be better at something or some skill will also be better than having an external motivation to earn more money. External motivations are goals that once reached take away all the desire to work and leave a person empty. So, when starting with something try to find intrinsic motivation.

Once you have defined that focus **it is now time to set goals**. When setting up a goal make sure you set an audacious goal. It is better when you set up a big goal and fail rather than setting up a small goal and failing. And this is why we teach kids to dream big and shoot for the stars. So set big goals and divide them into small milestones so that once you hit your small goals you get closer to your big goal as well. So, if you want to have a sales target of $20M it is better that you keep your target at $100M and work your way up using milestones rather than setting it up at $10M and failing miserably.

Lesson 2: For your real estate strategy to work you need leads, listings, and leverage

In the chapter *"The Three L's of The Millionaire Real Estate Agent"*, we learn that the success of any realtor depends on the ability to get three key objectives: **leads, listings and leverage**. In the real estate business, sales drive everything, and to maximize sales, you need to have maximum leads. When we backtrack the sales process, we would find that there would be no sales without listing and no listing without leads. Therefore, every sale comes down to the lead generation process. And if you have excess leads, you can have the freedom to select the best ones for you and try to convert those. On the other hand, there are few leads, and you do not have any choice but to miss your sales target.

Once you find enough leads, you can then move to have more listings. You will have the advantage of advertising your services to people who are trying to sell their homes rather than ones who are looking to buy one. And the reason for this is that it gives you more exposure. Think of all the potential buyers who would come to your viewings and would see your brands. They would become your potential customers.

Lastly, you need to be smart to **deploy people, tools, and services** to cut down your work and increase your income. You can do this by employing other real estate agents and taking your commission. You could also hire someone to manage all your administration work and manage all your marketing efforts. All these activities will give you more time to focus on the sales process. Now that you have everything planned, it is time to learn to execute those strategies effectively.

Lesson 3: Using available qualitative tools effectively can help you to execute your strategy

Until now we have looked at different strategies to run your real estate business, but now we will learn about four important tools that will aid you to grow your business successfully and sustainably. In

"The Four Fundamental Models of Real Estate Sales Success", we will learn about these four models.

First is **the economic model**, a tool that calculates the numbers you need to hit if you want to reach your target income. Once you have decided how much money you want to earn, the economic model helps you determine how many leads you need to have to reach this goal. For example, if your goal is to earn a revenue of $100K and you charge a 3% commission, you need to sell $3 million worth of properties. If on average the closing prize is $100,000, you need to sell 30 properties. And once you have the listing to conversion ratio, say for example 25% it would tell you to list 120 properties. And once you have the list the last step would be to calculate the number of leads you would need. If you have a lead to listing rate of 20%, you will need 600 leads to reach your goal. And that is the economic model. It's an immense help to figure out everything to reach your goal.

The second tool is the one that will **help to gain and maintain long-term clients** by getting those leads. Good lead generation happens when you have frequent contact with your potential client. But you do not want to be overly aggressive to the point that it becomes annoying. While contacting your potential client through email or call people are often aggressive and risk losing the lead, but when you meet those prospects face to face you can take it to the next level. You can reach out to them multiple times over a week and send them a letter along with a fridge magnet or a calendar as a gift. And for those people that you already know you can have a conversation or communication with them at least three to four times a month over birthdays, New Year, personal emails and other occasions.

These are powerful tools and next, we will learn about two more really powerful tools that you can use in your real estate journey.

Lesson 4: Use the budget and organizational models to help maximize your potential

The next two tools we will look at will help you define spending limits and help to take maximum organizational benefits.

The third tool **budget model** prevents you from using more money than you are making. As soon as possible you should only be spending money that your business is generating. Of course, this means that your growth curve is going to be slow, but it also means that the foundation on which it is set is also going to be very strong. And this strong foundation will help you build strength in the future. If you do not control your spending, the future of your business is going to be bleak. Just remember the dot-com boom when high growth expectations led companies to invest a lot of money to lose everything.

So then how do you know if it is okay to spend money to run after an opportunity? **Think about the streetlights**. When you see an opportunity to increase your revenue, you can increase your spending by having the green light. But when the light turns red, you will have to wait until your revenue grows and you can justify your spending. Once the revenue grows the light will turn green again and you can pursue further opportunities.

Whenever you have to decide which task to do and follow, **the organizational model will help your business**. It will help you hire new skilled people and eventually delegate some of your work so that you get some time to focus on the work that makes the most impact on your company. And the first person that you should hire should be someone who can manage administrative work for you so that you can focus on selling properties.

Always remember you get what you pay for and therefore it is better to pay more and get someone who is talented and motivated rather than someone who needs micromanagement to work. Think of it this way if you want to employ someone and they are asking for an extra $10,000 then they only need to make $1,000 extra every month to cover that cost. And this would be justifiable if the employee would free up more of your time so that you can do more sales. These tools, however, are just templates and your business will change as it grows. These tools will however help you make that journey smoother for you.

Lesson 5: The four models to help you pursue leads, listings, and leverages

In The chapter *"Sustaining a Solid Lead-Generation Program That Emphasises Marketing and Consistently Increases the Number of Leads"* we learn that once you have an established real estate business your goal would be to streamline and improve your strategies in getting leads, listings and leverage. Once again remember that you are in the business of generating leads, they define your real estate business. Whenever you are doing any kind of marketing all your efforts should go to generating more leads and this is exactly where a lead-generation model will help your business.

Leads are good only if you can convert them into listings. To make sure you hit the required number of listings, keep a track of your economic model. Check how many listings are required to reach your monthly goal and then convert them into the number of leads required. And if you do not do this, then you will never know how many more leads are required to hit your target and get your target income. It would be like trying to navigate an unknown city without a map. Also, **define your organizational model** so that it can give you more control over the work you do and give you more freedom.

Your organizational model should be according to your business need but only the need of today but what the business might need in the future too. You should know if you need to hire a person to work on an immediate need or need someone who is flexible and can adapt even the future need. Again, use the budget model along with your organizational model to make sure that you do not overshoot your budget. Implementing these models takes significant effort and having these models in place does not mean everything is fixed. It is this urge to self-improve and push to continually be better that will push you to modify these models accordingly.

Lesson 6: Failure and its acceptance is an important milestone in attaining personal success

Everyone wants to succeed, and this is a natural ambition of life, but what is also true is that you will only achieve success when you do not fear failure and start learning from failure. All of us are naturally fearful, but in business, you need to let go of this fear of failure. In the chapter *"Weighing Your Options— The Process Of Discovering What Works And Doesn't Work For You"*, we learn that we need to be ready for failures and learn what works and what does not work for our business from the failure itself.

In business as in real life, you will fail many times before you succeed. And you ought to have the perseverance to go hard enough to achieve your goal. So instead of having a negative approach and mindset, **see failure as a stepping stone to success** and as necessary for teaching.

It is important to accept failure, but it is equally important to conquer self-doubt, especially those self-doubts that are not based on truth and facts. People used to think it was impossible to go to the moon before Buzz Aldrin and Neil Armstrong did it. And once they did this, psychologically and technically everyone knew it was possible and we saw many countries sending people to the moon. Before this ever happened, many people thought that it was impossible to send people to the moon.

In real estate, a lot of your success is about visualizing yourself as a victor and only a few can do this without any self-doubt. But only the greats know that there is no finish line. You always strive to be a better version of yourself.

Lesson 7: Work on the business rather than in the business

While the most skilled agents have some limits on their time charges, there is no actual limit to how successful your real estate business can be. Although you have the most successful business and close the biggest deal, your most valuable asset will always be your time.

In the chapter *"Active vs Passive income"* we learn that when the time comes when you decide to earn more passive income from your business, **you must decide to work on your business** and not necessarily make sales for yourself. For example, you might come across a time when you do not want to expand the business and a passive income of $100,000 a year might be enough. This is the way you can achieve that. If right now you are making $300,000 per year, you can pay a business manager anywhere between $100,000 to $150,000 and hit that target. And this would not require any kind of work from your side.

As a teenager, the author used to charge $15 to mow the lawn and as his business grew, he hired his friends to help him. He used to pay them $10 and keep the rest $5. Thus, he earned it without doing any active work. It is possible to earn millions by creating multiple businesses and hiring managers to handle them. To become a **successful real estate agent**, you can define and strategize your business using the four models, define your target passive income and then determine the number of agencies you need to reach to reach your goal. At that scale, your organization would be big and would include managers, administrators, and people who could help both sellers and buyers. This model can then be replicated in other units and entities as well. Once you make that decision to switch to a passive income, your focus will be on how those decisions affect your business in the present and future.

Lesson 8: You need a high level of focus for long-term success

Why do some people produce entirely different results even after getting the same kind of training? In the chapter *"Create a Personal Plan And Then Make Process Your Focus"*, we learn that a major difference between successful people and people who are very successful is the way and direction in which they focus their energy. As a manager, you cannot focus on every remote aspect of your business and you need to focus on what is most important for your business.

Why is it that, even after receiving the same training, two people will produce entirely different results?

While working, keep the Pareto principle in mind. 80% of your success and outcome come from 20% of your time and resources. Therefore, when you are getting started, you might have to work with many parties to keep yourself afloat. However, once you have established your business, you can start picking the leads that are the most important ones.

You do not need to run around and focus on everything, you should be focusing on the main leads and let your agents focus on the other leads. As your agents bring you more business, you will still make money. This way you focus on other parts of your business. The important lesson here is to **focus on your goals and success** and not feel too bothered by failure. You can achieve success in many different ways, but one thing is certain: to win in any way, you need to be highly focused.

Conclusion

Here is the conclusion of The Millionaire Real Estate Agent By Gary Keller

In real estate, your success comes down to leads, listings, and leverages. Once you have your business up and running based on these principles, you can change your focus. You can try to grow your business while nurturing other agents to bring more business for you. All the while you should be planning and budgeting based on your earnings and the financial goals that you have set. Take help from the economic model to determine the leads you need to reach your goal. Once you follow these results, you would be seeing results instantly

earnings and the financial goals that you have set. Take help from the economic model to determine the leads you need to reach your goal. Once you follow these results, you would be seeing results instantly

100+ SUCCESSFUL REAL ESTATE AGENT AFFIRMATIONS – READ IT DAILY TO GET BEST RESULT

1. I am a successful real estate agent.
2. My success is my biggest priority.
3. I am ready to do what it takes to succeed.
4. I understand that by helping more clients, I become more successful.
5. I love helping my clients.
6. My determination allows me to sell any property that I want.
7. I am building my destiny the way I like it.
8. I take the initiative when it is needed.
9. I feel confident when I am selling.
10. I work smart and **use the right tools** in my business.
11. I can deliver eye-opening open houses.
12. I can sell properties quickly and with ease.
13. I have faith in my abilities.
14. I exude confidence and charisma.
15. I am an expert in this field.

16.   My skills are improving day by day.

17.   Nobody can compete with my skills.

18.   My passion is unrivaled.

19.   I love the work that I do as a realtor.

20.   I found my calling while working in real estate.

21.   I am charming and charismatic around my clients.

22.   My clients appreciate my passion and dedication.

23.   They know that I only want the best for them.

24.   My clients trust me quickly.

25.   I am **honest and genuine** with my clients.

26.   My clients appreciate my work and recommend me to other people.

27.   My clients feel satisfied with my work.

28.   My service is considered valuable.

29.   I attract new clients quickly.

30.   I achieve all my business goals quickly.

31.   I make new partnerships when it is needed.

32.   My business is thriving.

33.   My colleagues in this field are impressed by me.

34.   With every passing day, I become more successful.

35.   I am closing more deals than I can count.

36.   The sky's the limit for me.

37.   I have **unlimited potential** that fuels my work.

38.   Other people love to work with me.

39.   My talents lie in buying and selling property.

40.   I have become a pro in this field.

41.   Other people seek my advice.

42.   I inspire other people to achieve their business goals.

43.   I love helping people find properties that they need.

44. I am learning important lessons on the way.
45. I allow my mistakes to guide me.
46. I do not give up easily.
47. I overcome challenges with courage and confidence.
48. Nothing and nobody can **stop me from achieving my goals**.
49. I enjoy my work immensely.
50. I feel fortunate to work as a realtor.
51. I provide outstanding service to my clients.
52. My clients feel excited to work with me.
53. They know I will solve all their problems.
54. I can find the best deals for my clients.
55. My clients feel lucky to have me as their realtor.
56. I have done fantastic work in the past, and I will do even better in the future.
57. I am not fixated on my mistakes.
58. I am proud of the work I've done so far.
59. I take charge of my life and **always perform to the best** of my abilities.
60. I know that I'm responsible for my success and my happiness.
61. I know what needs to be done to succeed.
62. I have worked hard to gain people's trust.
63. My business is growing every single day.
64. My career has been extraordinarily successful.
65. I know the market exceptionally well.
66. I find the best buyers and sellers for my work.
67. I am at ease talking to different people and attracting new clients.
68. My clients are loyal to me.

69. My work is thriving thanks to my efforts.
70. I make the most out of every opportunity that I get.
71. **I start every day motivated** to be the best.
72. I am sure that every day will be a great day.
73. I am attracting success for myself.
74. I can see my net worth grow.
75. The number in my bank account is growing steadily.
76. My business has made me financially secure.
77. I do not rely on anybody else.
78. I am working independently and in control of my decisions.
79. I am a natural when it comes to selling and closing deals.
80. I have gained immense experience over the years and am now an expert in this field.
81. My talents and expertise are put to good use.
82. The **fear of failure cannot stop me** from achieving my goals.
83. I am ambitious and have great plans for my future.
84. I can solve any problem presented in front of me.
85. I have a positive attitude regarding my business.
86. I always see the silver lining in difficult situations.
87. My clients are attracted to my positivity and my optimism.
88. I am enthusiastic about working in this field and doing my best.
89. My enthusiasm makes me an exceptional realtor.
90. I can see the different possibilities in a property.
91. My goal is to **help people achieve their dreams.**
92. Other people find it easy to rely on me.
93. I am welcoming toward all my clients.
94. I can turn any stranger into my client.

95. I am working hard to achieve success.

96. I am pursuing my goals relentlessly.

97. I am the best real estate agent.

98. I can outsmart all my competitors.

99. I seek out the best real estate opportunities for myself.

100. I always overdeliver excellent service to my clients

101. I am an **effective and strategic negotiator**.

102. I am in control of my life and my business.

103. I have built my reputation as a successful realtor.

104. I am known for my success rates.

105. I am grateful for everything I have achieved so far.

REAL ESTATE LISTING LEADS RESOURCES

Market to FSBOs

FSBO, in other words, For Sale by Owner homes are homes where the owners have decided to sell their houses themselves as opposed to listing with an agent. They are most sought in real estate since they have previously expressed an interest in selling their house.

For many of them, selling by themselves may be quite frustrating since they lack the requisite expertise in staging, pricing their homes, closing deals with potential buyers, and dealing with all the contingencies arising from the contract's documentation.

*On average, For Sale by Owner homes are **sold for twenty-six percent less than houses** where agents are involved, which defeats their primary purpose of not wanting an agent to save cost.*

This information is probably not known to them, and as a seller, it's your job to inform them.

Most of them put up signages on the properties they want to sell, so by driving around your neighborhood, you might find a few of the FSBO homes.

You can also look them up on Craigslist since many offer their homes there. If you have a small budget, RedX, Landvoice, and Offers contain contact information and property data for a large number of **FSBO leads**.

With their contact information available, you should start cold-calling them. When interacting with those owners, you should sell yourself to them by promoting principles that address reasons why they'd rather sell their property themselves.

You can tell them that you could sell their homes for them, get your commission and still hand them more money than they could have had if they sold it themselves because of your expertise in pricing.

You can also offer them low commission rates to entice them to list with you. **Don't forget to keep touching base** with them time and again.

Expired listings

Expired listings are properties that were unable to sell before their expiration dates. They provide an opportunity to identify a genuine vendor who is willing and ready to sell.

To get expired listings, you must be the first agent to contact the homeowner after their listing has expired. **Retrieve expired listing lists from the MLS**. Be aware that these sellers are likely dissatisfied with their existing agent, frustrated that their home hasn't sold, and are probably stressed.

Sign up for real estate prospecting services like RedX and Landvoice to get lists of expired listings. These services look for expired properties through the MLS system and offer real contact details.

Although these services are not free, they will save you time and effort over manually looking for them.

Regardless of how you obtain your expired listings, start the conversation by letting them know you sympathize with their difficulties and mention a few things you would have done differently to sell their house quickly.

It's increasingly possible that **another agent may contact them first the longer you wait**. A great strategy to take advantage of sellers in trouble is to get in touch with homeowners who are trying to sell their properties or have tried and failed to do so.

Divorce leads

Don't pass judgment just yet. Competition for low-hanging fruit leads is usually fierce in almost any farm region.

Consider the following questions:

- Do you want leads who are genuinely interested in selling?
- What about leads who have a court order compelling them to sell their home? What about motivating leads?

If you want to generate and close more leads, you must learn to think outside the box. But we've already done that for you! **Working divorce leads** may be the ideal lead generation approach if you have plenty of patience and empathy.

Divorce leads have the potential to be as productive as they are unpleasant to consider. However, they are mostly forced to sell (via a court order). Divorced leads necessitate tact and compassion. As you may expect, these clients aren't delighted with their current situation. But if you can locate and appeal to them, you'll have a steady stream of highly motivated clients.

You can even **obtain the RCS-D** (Real Estate Collaboration Specialist – Divorce) credential to demonstrate to prospective divorce customers that you know your stuff and mean business.

Invest in Sphere Influence

One of the best ways to get seller leads is by having good connections with people both offline and online. Your sphere of influence includes family, friends, colleagues, and past clients.

About 42% of people who sold their houses through real estate agents got to know about those agents through referrals.

By building the right connections with your sphere of influence, you would be on their lips once anyone comes to them for recommendations. **You can host events** and invite those within your sphere of influence to generate referral listing leads. This would further enhance your relationship with them.

Always show up at community events, actively participate and share your business cards with the other attendees. By doing this, you'll be announcing your presence in that locality.

Your previous clients should be followed up using **client relationship management software**. This software makes it very easy for you to store the contact information of all your previous clients, and you will use that to call, send texts and keep in touch with them.

Using this strategy, anytime they have a family, friend, or colleague searching for a listing agent, you'll be the first they'll remember because you've always been present.

Invite Absentee Owners

An absentee owner is a person, group, or entity that has a certain property but does not reside within the locality of the said property. While not every absentee owner will like to sell their property, there's a high likelihood that most individuals would. This is because it can be challenging to maintain an additional property.

Absentee owners are **nice targets for real estate agents** who are wondering which type of leads have the best conversion rate into listings since there are millions of absentee owner houses in the market.

Finding absentee owners is just as simple as reviewing tax records and knowing whose residential address does not match the prospective property. With property radar, you can find the social media handles of these owners.

Another easy way is by buying an absentee owner list from Listsource, Zillow, or Boldleads. After getting your list, the next thing to do is to start your mailing campaign. Inside these emails should be details that portray you as an expert in the business of selling houses.

Your previous success stories and the current market stats and trends should form part of the content you'll be sending out to them. You can also get them to **visit your website using postcards**. This website should be loaded with valuable information which will make them continually visit and anticipate future updates and information from you.

A deal closed on this lead will net you a lot of money, which is why many people are jumping on it.

Contact Pre-foreclosed Owner

Pre-foreclosure is a time usually within three to six months that starts when a borrower is in default of a mortgage payment. In August, 34,501 properties had foreclosure filings, with 3,900 completed the same month. This shows that a whole lot is going on in the real estate industry as it pertains to foreclosures. Most debtors who can't afford to pay are often in a hurry to sell off their properties to avoid foreclosing.

As non-professionals, they are often distressed and frustrated about how to go about selling their homes, and that's where you come in.

As a realtor, you should look out for this group of people because they are more likely to welcome your offer to sell their property.

To find the details of pre-foreclosed homes, you should **visit the office of your city's county recorder or their official website online**. The details include the address of the property and the name of the owner.

With this information, you can physically reach out to the owner, obtain their email and phone numbers, explain how you can help sell their property if they decide to and follow up with emails and phone calls.

Also, the local newspapers always publish the information of those people whose homes are pre-foreclosed in their legal section, so you should buy a few newspapers, get the needed details and start calling them. With the right words and approach, you'd be getting a lot of listings from these leads.

Social media ads

A paid social media ad is a technique for presenting commercials or sponsored marketing messages on well-known social media platforms while aiming to reach a certain niche market. You should run specifically targeted lead ads on Instagram, Facebook, or Twitter to reach your desired market.

Facebook lead ads contain forms that enable advertisers to gather client information while providing interaction options, including newsletter subscriptions, demo requests, or contest registration.

Your content should be appealing, concise, and informative to encourage more people to sign these forms. Incentives such as giveaways, discounted products, or shopping vouchers would also encourage more people to sign the forms.

Twitter advertising can significantly increase traffic to your website. Like other forms of advertising, it necessitates knowledge of your target market's demographics and habits.

Statistics suggest that consumers spend 26% more time watching ads on Twitter than on other platforms and that it has higher engagements than other social media platforms.

Twitter ads can even offer you more than Facebook and Instagram ads with their interesting marketing concepts. By sending customized messages to people based on the topics they connect and engage with on Twitter, Twitter interest targeting enables you to participate in the many vibrant communities on the platform.

REAL ESTATE ADVERTISING STRATEGIES TO ENGAGE WITH TARGET AUDIENCE

Always Use Professional Photos

Your career as a realtor relies a lot on the use of photos, which are probably more important than property descriptions. This is why you should never underestimate and take for granted the undefeatable power of photos.

Statistics revealed that most homeowners today go online when searching for properties to buy or sell. But do you know the first thing people notice on your website or listings? It's photos! **Photos can help sell a house faster** and sometimes, for even more money.

On the other hand, if you only use small photos that you probably captured with your phone camera, you cannot expect these to encourage someone to even glance at your description. Thus, always equip your real estate brochures with professional-looking photos.

Professional photographers will have the necessary know-how on what it takes to put a house in the spotlight through proper lighting, angles, and editing. While it is often the best and most recommended option to **hire a photographer** to take the photos you need, you can always do it on your own with a bit of research and study and a good quality camera in case your budget is a bit limited.

Don't forget that good photos will evoke and associate more positive emotions with the house, so always use them to your advantage.

Offer Virtual Tours to Your Clients

While photos are great, there is something else that does better, and this is none other than a virtual tour! Virtual tours are 360-degree panoramas that are an exciting and one-of-a-kind way to let people immerse and imagine themselves in a room or yard.

Virtual tours are a great way to **showcase your best properties**. The viewers get the chance to look side to side in any direction to check every single detail and aspect of the place.

You can also embed these virtual tours on your official website and let them impress all your visitors. Everyone prefers to work with experts, and virtual tours can definitely help make look like one.

Come Up with Smart Listing Descriptions

Regardless of the materials that you use for your real estate agent advertising efforts, your number one goal here is to stand out from the rest. How can you do that? Clever writing should always be your priority here. A good story is always at the forefront of a good real estate advertising strategy.

Always come up with **enticing listing descriptions** for every property that you want to rent or sell. These descriptions should highlight unique amenities and the best features. Include new improvements and add words that can make the readers imagine what it would feel like to actually live in the house.

If a house is the main highlight of your real estate brochure, make sure a feeling is connected with the object, such as describing how the home can serve as a safe haven after work. Smart listing descriptions can help transport readers to the setting you are describing, increasing the chances that a potential client will grab the phone to get in touch with you.

Avoid shocking or strange descriptions, though, that might have the opposite effect on your readers. Instead, use words that will make the descriptions linger in their memory for a long time in a positive way.

The internet is now filled with lots of creative real estate descriptions so walk the extra mile and don't be lazy.

Try Blogging

Blogs work as a more indirect approach compared to other real estate agent advertising strategies like postcards. While you won't see results immediately, the effort will be worth it sooner or later.

A professional real estate may take some maintenance effort on your part, but all the time and work invested in it will pay off in the long run.

Having your own blog is also the perfect opportunity for you to **showcase your experience as a realtor**, drive more business to your door, attract more website traffic, and let everyone see your knowledge of the real estate market.

Add Customer Testimonials to Your Website

Reviews and testimonials on your real estate website can generate more social proof to make you and your business seem more reliable. People often follow others who are just like them. Every time they read about someone who was in a situation similar to theirs, they will pay more attention and heed the advice of that person.

Testimonials are like the **bulletproof vest of your real estate advertising strategy**. They don't just work because they can also get rid of any doubt in people's minds. It is how testimonials work so don't forget to add some that come from your past clients with relatable stories.

Use Videos to Your Advantage

Videos are another fantastic tool for marketing for all types and sizes of businesses. However, they work extra great in the real estate field. **Create videos that present all your best properties** so you can attract more new leads and show off your listings in an engaging and striking way.

Put Ads in Online Newspapers

Ads in online newspapers continue to provide value to realtors even to this day of the modern digital age. All you have to do is look for a trusted local newspaper that can bring in more quality leads.

Never assume that newspapers are a real estate advertising strategy that already belongs to the Middle Ages. They are more than that and still work well. Despite being a rather traditional strategy, it is still very prevalent now. Many people continue to read newspapers, whether physical or online, to find helpful information so be sure to add them to your advertising arsenal.

You can use online newspapers for promoting your real estate business by **harnessing the power of this community**. Once people read your ads, they will feel more interested to learn more about you and your offerings.

Don't Leave Out Your Email Signature

Your email signature is a must to add to your emails to make people recall you better. Just make sure that your email signature is simple but includes pertinent contact information, such as your name, company name and job title, mobile phone number, office phone number, and link to your website. You can also choose to add your social media profiles if you like.

Real estate business cards can also be good examples of **effective signatures you can use as part of your real estate advertising effort**. Business cards offer clients a glimpse of your professional self. So don't forget to always have your business cards with you no matter where you go.

While business cards might have been in existence for some time now, there is no sign that they will disappear anytime soon, and they shouldn't either. Business cards can make a great first impression as it reveals what type of professional you are. Just like your email signature, your business cards should also contain your important contact details so people can reach out to you right away.

Harness the Power of Flipbooks

Turn your real estate presentations or brochures into Flipbooks to make them more interesting and attractive. Flipbooks are super easy to make, are shareable, and look gorgeous. You can also **embed Flipbooks on your site** if you like.

You can use existing templates for your Flipbooks or develop them from scratch. You can also add links and videos to your real estate flipbook to better present your listings.

Try Google Ads

Google Ads is probably the most popular way that realtors can use to start their PPC advertising campaigns. With Google being the most widely used search engine in the world, it is almost expected that it also has the biggest impact on today's real estate industry. It is where sellers and buyers go to search for local realtors and listings, which can help you get the **best results for your ads campaign**.

Google advertising using PPC works like a bidding system where the users set up their bids on a particular keyword. Every time a user looks for that specific term, the Google algorithm will decide the keywords to show to the user. Different factors affect this decision such as how you set up and optimize your landing page for a clear and better user experience, the relevance of keywords that your ads use, the quality score of Google for your ads, and the ad copy's quality itself.

Respond Quickly and Informatively

As a realtor, being able to respond fast to queries can make or break your business. Make sure you always have constant access to your email, which can be easily achieved by setting it up on your smartphone.

Make it a regular habit to check notifications and your email inbox. **Respond to every query you receive as soon as possible** even if you might not have a lot of spare time to come up with a lengthy reply. You can use these prompt replies to encourage leads to get in touch with you to schedule a meeting or call you later for additional details.

Don't Forget to Retarget

For most people, it often takes anywhere between two weeks to four months of research before they reach a final decision on what property to buy. You can use retargeting to leverage this window of opportunity.

Don't forget to remind all your site visitors about you and your services and encourage them to come back for more. Since these people also showed or expressed their interest in your site listings, it means they are already considered qualified leads.

By **setting up a retargeting campaign**, people will continue to see your ads even if they are on other sites. It saves you from wasting your money on people who might not even be the least interested in your services. With the higher conversion rates associated with retargeting, it only makes sense to make the most out of them.

Have Targeted Facebook Ads in Place

While newspaper ads work well and are good in what they are meant to do, online ads are much better in this digital world. In fact, running a **Facebook campaign** for just a few dollars a day can already generate good leads using the right ads and the right campaign settings.

If you have never tried doing it before, it is actually quite simple. All you have to do is choose a few houses with different prices and come up with an interesting ad or headline text. Your headline must be interesting enough to make them stand out from the rest of the usual boring ads. Add photos of houses and **choose first-time homebuyers or renters as your audience**.

Aside from targeting custom audiences on Facebook by adding the Facebook Pixel tag, remarketing can also be done by targeting your website visitors or flipbook viewers, for example.

Make the Most Out of YouTube Ads

If your listings are already using some great videos, using them for your **YouTube ads campaign** can make them even more powerful. To make them more effective, try limiting the audience only to viewers in your area or city.

Since YouTube is one of the biggest platforms right now, your ads will be seen by more people, and a good percentage of them will likely click the ads and hopefully contact you to view a property.

Boost Your Social Media Posts

If your Facebook page has low engagement rates, it might be high time for you to consider boosting your posts. To do this, you can add a photo of a house, a short but catchy description, and your website URL.

After you post this just like what you do with regular Facebook posts, don't forget to click the boost button. You can then choose your target audience afterward. Choose a local audience and target only those whom you think will show interest in the type of property you have. The good news here is that you don't need a large budget to make a big difference.

Attract Leads from Craigslist

Yes, you've read that right. Craigslist can also work wonders in generating qualified real estate leads, not to mention that you can use it with no need to pay for anything. It makes it an **effective tool for your real estate advertising strategy**, especially if you consider the immense and extensive popularity of the platform. Just don't forget to do your research to find guides that can help you generate more leads with Craigslist so you can expect better results.

Maintain a Facebook Page

Now more than ever, it is expected for all businesses to have their own dedicated Facebook page. It doesn't matter what your real estate advertising might be, a Facebook page is something your venture can never survive without.

Don't worry since it won't cost you a dime to make one, not to mention that the process is also super easy. Use your Facebook page to promote all your listings and engage with your audience at the same time.

Use Lead Generators

The use of lead generators is something that some realtors claim to have helped them succeed with their ventures. Others, however, think otherwise. But whether you like or hate these lead generators, it cannot be denied how realtors widely use these websites, so they also deserve to be mentioned in any list of real estate advertising strategies. Realtor.com. Trulia and Zillow are some of the perfect and most popular examples of these lead generators.

Spruce Up Your LinkedIn Profile

Facebook has already been mentioned several times as a critical part of your real estate advertising campaigns. But despite being effective, using just one is not enough sometimes. Although you don't necessarily have to use all the different social media platforms out there, LinkedIn is another site where you should be in addition to Facebook.

LinkedIn is the **top networking site for professionals** including realtors like yourself. It is the best place to be if you want to grow your network while serving as a great online business card. See to it that you fill in a summary of your experience, education, and other important details. If you are willing to go that extra mile, you can also start your own LinkedIn company page.

Create or Be a Part of Facebook and WhatsApp Real Estate Groups

Local WhatsApp and Facebook real estate groups are like a goldmine, so try to find out if your local area has **dedicated WhatsApp or Facebook groups** and join them.

You can even create some groups yourself. If you already have an existing community, regardless of its size, you can unite everyone under Facebook's banner. With the internet now filled with all kinds of groups, including Facebook, you wouldn't have a hard time attracting more members. Find the right spot and you will be good to go.

Tweet It

Twitter is another equally popular and massive social media platform that realtors should use to their advantage. Don't worry if you aren't too familiar with tweets because you can always look at how other bigger real estate companies are using Twitter and making it work for their business.

Create Professional Business Cards

Professional business cards should always be in your pockets as they are the simplest but most effective forms of real estate advertising. By keeping them handy all the time, you can distribute them when and as needed. Again, make sure your **business cards exude professionalism** and ensure that all your contact details are updated and correct.

Distribute door hangers for Effective Door to Door Marketing

Put on your running shoes and start distributing door hangers within your neighborhood for literal and figurative door-to-door marketing.

Optimize Your Website for Local Searches

When it comes to real estate agent advertising, **studying SEO is a must** if you want to increase your chances of getting found on major search engines. Local traffic should be your priority, with your main keywords including the name of the area or city you work in.

Continue to Help Even After the Sale

Just because you already made a sale doesn't mean it's the end. Make yourself available and help your clients as much as you can after you receive your commission.

Don't Forget Your Former Clients

Your previous clients might be your **biggest and most important referrals**. Happy clients will be more than willing to refer you to others.

Increase Your Leads with 360 Ad Templates

Get your hands on 360 real estate ads that are professionally designed that you can use to attract more clients and leads. If you want to save more money and time, https://soldouthouses.com/adtemplates can give you exactly just that. Tweak things around from colors to pictures and text with no need to hire a designer or pay for Photoshop.

REAL ESTATE COLD CALLING TECHNIQUES THAT REALLY WORK (WITH SCRIPT)

Do you want to Cold Call like a Pro realtor and land reliable clients with just a call?

As in any other sector, cold calling is one of the most recommended and established methods of lead generation in real estate. Unfortunately, this is also one of the worst nightmares that realtors have. The most difficult thing for most realtors is to convince someone to choose you when they know nothing about you.

However, preparing and executing proven real estate cold-calling scripts will help you close more sales than you ever imagined. You don't need supernatural abilities to make cold calls that convert. Your preparation and mode of delivery will determine your success.

So, to help you prepare like a Pro, we have compiled **5 Real Estate Cold Calling Techniques** that really work with Scripts. If you are fed up with not knowing what to say on the call with a potential client, go through this article and become a Pro at cold calling.

Cold calling Script for For Sale by Owner (FSBO) leads

Many times, homeowners overprice their homes. They believe they could have gotten more. However, most of them do not know that you as a realtor can assist them and save them the stress of unyielding results.

You will demonstrate to homeowners that they can get more from the sale of their homes if they list with you. You're not just tossing out statistics but also backing up your claim with **verifiable market research**.

So initiate the dialogue and ensure that you establish, build, and solidify trust with them as soon as possible. Here's how you start the dialogue:

Hello, this is Mr. George from Soldouthouses real estate agency phoning to inquire about your property. Are you the legal owner of the property?

Great! Is this a good time to go through everything in detail?

I noticed your listing and found your house at so and so location is for sale. I want to clarify your precise asking price for the property.

Wait for your potential client to respond and give you further details about the house. Then continue with this:

I see. How long have you had the house on the market?

*Alright. Before making this contact, I'd like to point out that I **performed some market research** on the properties in your neighborhood, and my homework revealed some fascinating facts.*

In the last five years, residences in your neighborhood have sold for an average of so and so amount. Furthermore, they sold in so and so days.

This information will let your client know how informed you are about the house and the neighborhood. This will make him or her rely on you.

*A **well-structured marketing plan** will help you speed up the process and sell your home for the price it deserves. I want to assist you in doing the same.*

Are you interested in seeing a marketing strategy that I created just for your home?

You can now continue the conversation from here.

Cold calling script for heavy sales leads in the neighborhood

This sort of cold-calling script works incredibly well if the client does not currently live in the house. This is because they have lost touch with the current local trends by not living in that particular neighborhood, so they have information about how the real estate market has been in that region for the previous few years or months. This is where you will come in as a realtor, and let them know that information.

However, while using this cold-calling real estate script, you may encounter a lot of "no's."

People may be wary of the high costs you offer, but if you are genuine and your quotation is supported by thorough market research, there is nothing that can prevent you from convincing your prospect to accept you.

So how do you do that? This script makes it easier:

Hello, this is Mr. George from soldouthouses real estate agency phoning to inquire about your property on so and so street. Are you the legal owner of the property?

Two beautiful residences like yours have sold in your area in the last two months.

Mention the sale prices.

I see that the property has been vacant for quite some time. Given the recent increase in the prices of this area, whether you rent or sell it, you may make a terrific secondary income stream from it.

Are you willing to perform either of these?

This cold call script will assist you in gauging their reaction as to what they want to accomplish. Even if they decide not to sell, you might assist them in finding someone to lease their home. In any case, you may earn a lot of money.

Cold calling Script for Online Buyer Lead

When leads visit your real estate company's website and fill out their wants and criteria online, they are often waiting for you and your organization to contact them.

In such circumstances, your organization usually sends them an email containing the lead's requested information, but the lead rarely checks their email and even when they do, they do not always send back their feedback…

Now you see why doing a **follow-up cold call is very important**! If you don't follow up, you lose a key customer as a result.

So in such cases, it's a good idea to phone them a few days after you send them the email with the information they wanted. This script will be perfect for that purpose:

Hello, this is Mr. George from soldouthouses real estate agency calling to inquire about the online form you completed on our website regarding your interest in purchasing a home. Do you recall completing the form?

Great! This is a good time to discuss it in depth.

Awesome! I am ensuring that you received the information you asked for because we did not receive a response to the email we sent.

I've been in this industry for so and so years. I see you want property in so and so area. This is an excellent neighborhood option. I sold a property in this neighborhood two months ago at _____ price.

Mention all the great things that have happened in that neighborhood and the quality of the neighborhood. Then finalize things with this question:

Can we meet tomorrow and talk about this in person?

You will be able to create trust with the consumer by demonstrating that **you have expertise in selling properties in the area** they are interested in using this cold call script. This way, your prospect knows they're in good hands.

Reaching out to them proactively demonstrates that you care about them and want to help them get the most out of their home.

Cold calling Script for Expired Listing

It is complex to sell a property. And it is extremely common for prospects to offer their homes for sale on their own, but even after a significant period has passed, it is very possible that they were unable to sell them.

This depresses and frustrates the homeowner. They know they need to learn how to go about selling it.

The script for **cold calling on an expired listing** can help a real estate agent to convince a homeowner to relist their property and give it another chance.

If you use the correct phrases, you can get the homeowner enthused about attempting to sell the house again. This is what to say:

Hello, this is Mr. George from soldouthouses real estate agency. I'm calling about the property at so and so location. Are you the lawful owner of this property?

I see you put your house up for sale around a year ago; however, the listing has now expired. Is now a suitable time to have a discussion?

Awesome! Are you planning to relist the property for sale?

*I appreciate your concern. But let me assure you that your house is a fantastic property in a fantastic location, which is why I am interested in **assisting you in selling it**. What was the highest offer you ever received?*

I see. Did the purchasers identify any major difficulties that prevented them from purchasing the property?

Alright. I see a lot of room for development here and based on the current market analysis I conducted in your neighborhood; I can obtain a higher price for your house.

I sold a home on your street two months ago. You will likely know the place. I negotiated a fantastic bargain for the vendor.

Mention the property's selling price.

Would you want to meet with me to explore how we might change our sales approach to assist you in getting the most out of your property?

Carrot Dangle Cold Calling Script

Carrot Dangling is when you have buyers but no properties to show them in the location they want, and having a cold-calling script is the best approach to making those buyers your clients...

Many times, homeowners are just seeking for the appropriate agent to come along and assist them in selling their homes. You can contact these homeowners in the neighborhood to see if they want to sell their homes.

You can inform the owners that buyers are willing to pay a fair price for their homes. In this manner, you may get homeowners enthused about selling their property, which they first felt **would not fetch a high price**, Doing this you will serve as the link between the homeowners and buyers who are willing to buy the houses.

This is how you can make that cold call:

Hello, this is Mr. George from soldouthouses real estate agency phoning to inquire about your property at so and so location. Are you the legal owner of the property?

Great! I have numerous purchasers that are keen on your house. Do you want to sell your property right now?

I have several purchasers, the most important of which is at so and so price.

Mention the highest-paying buyer you have for the property.

That's 36% higher than the current market value of your home.

You may be wondering why they're prepared to pay more than the market price.

Here you mention the reasons and detail the advantages of their property.

I appreciate your concern. It is complex to sell your home. But could we meet and talk about it further, and I could answer all of your concerns?

Script for Seller Leads Who Do Not Want to Hire Realtors

You might have encountered some people who are bent on not using a realtor. You might be wondering how to convince them to use a realtor to do the job for them. Here is the secret!

Firstly, you must know that your goal is to **understand the prospect's lack of interest** in using a real estate agent. This will help you to know exactly how to enlighten them. They might have had bad experiences in the past. You need to persuade them that cooperating with you would be advantageous for them and will increase their chances of selling their house easily and at a better price.

For instance, financial considerations are mostly why people sell their properties. So they always want to make the most money from the sale of their property. They often steer clear of real estate brokers because they may have had bad experiences in the past or believe that doing so would be expensive and will cost them extra money.

Now that you are aware of what they have in mind, your job as a real estate agent is to persuade them that you can help them save more money or obtain a better bargain.

This script will show you how you will do that using empathy:

"Hello, I just saw your listing on a real estate website, and I have a few inquiries about the house you are selling. Do you own the property?

I am Mr. George from soldouthouses real estate agency. I phoned you because I have a few clients seeking houses similar to the one you're selling; please tell me what your asking price is.

That's fantastic. Do you currently work with a real estate agent?

Okay. I wouldn't want you to go through the same things you did in the past. Although I am not requesting you pay for my service, I want to provide you with some information to enable you to negotiate a better price if indeed it's something you desire.

Alright. Let's talk more over a cup of coffee. Do you find this date convenient?"

The wise realtor has done it again. Your potential client will likely become your trusted client because he realizes you are not after just the money, but you want something better for him.

A script for expired listing seller leads

We all know that expired listings are a sign that things are not going well with the sale but when you want to talk about this with your lead, don't jump to conclusions or be quick to **criticize the owner or an earlier realtor** for their approaches.

At this point, clients typically feel sad since the previous transaction did not go through, and several agents are phoning the seller due to the expired listing. If you jump to a conclusion, It will make your chances of getting the appointments slim.

Understand exactly what went wrong with the listing, especially the client's perspective. And when you know this, switching from an emotional to a business setting is super simple. Ask open-ended questions such as, "From your perspective, what attributes should the agent have to effectively represent you?" and "What steps were taken by the prior agent?" The answers will get you the information you need.

You should also try to provide **free marketing advice** as a way to establish trust between you and your lead. Too much to take in? Do not worry we have this script for you:

Hello ...am I speaking with Mr. Mark?

Hello, I'm from soldouthouses real estate agency.

You probably have realized that your home appeared on our computer as an expired listing.

When do you intend to conduct interviews with potential realtors to sell your home?

Where would you move to if you sold this house?

How soon must you move?

What do you believe prevented the sale of your house?

How did you choose the previous agent that you listed with?

What did that agent do that you thought was effective?

What do you think they ought to have done?

What will you expect from the next agent you select?

Have you decided on a realtor with whom to work already?

Now that I am acquainted with what you want, are you acquainted with the methods I employ to sell homes? If so, I'd like you to consider me to sell your house.

What time would be most suitable for us to meet to discuss how we can help?

The best script usually contains many questions and helps you as a realtor to do little talking and more of **understanding your potential client**. This is because the likelihood that the prospective seller will do business with you increases if they like you and your services. Also, the prospective seller will be willing to conduct business with you if you do less talking and more listening. They will feel in charge.

Best Real Estate Scripts for Buyer Leads:

Script for Warming Up Internet Leads

Following up with online buyer leads differs from other forms of real estate script techniques because you often know more about the person you're contacting.

For instance, you could know what listings caught their attention or how long they stayed on the website, and you must know how to utilize this knowledge. Also, remember that sometimes the **best timing to use the information** is more important than the information itself. Just as we did in the earlier scripts, this one is more of a discussion between you and the Buyer lead:

Hello, Mr. Mark! I work for soldouthouses real estate agency and I am Mr. George. I hope you are doing great.

You appear to be planning to buy a house soon! I'd love to learn more about your requirements. Do you currently have like 3 minutes?

Have you read the report about your property?

In the upcoming six months, are you looking to purchase a property?

Where are you moving?

Are you and your family moving to this home?

What would you say about your perfect home? Mention things like the rooms, bathrooms, ranch, split-level, or condo.

How much are you prepared to spend?

Do you currently work with an agent?

Are you pre-qualified by a lender?

Can I send you an email with more properties that suit your criteria?

Is [insert Buyer lead email] still a reliable method of contact?

I appreciate you taking the time out of your day to speak with me. By [insert date/time], I'll email you information about a couple of homes. Do you have any questions for me regarding house purchases?

Please let me know your opinions on these issues and the initial properties I provide you. What time would be ideal for reaching you tomorrow to have a detailed conversation on what you would love to have?

I am grateful for your time and I'm eager to speak with you soon. What time would be convenient for you?"

Scripts to Score Leads from Open Houses

Experienced real estate agents know that holding an open house rarely results in a straight sale. If that's your only goal, you probably need to catch up on a lot of things going on in the industry.

One of the few actions that highly productive realtors perform during open house hosting is finding potential buyers for other houses. Well it does not just happen, you will have to do some talking and this script is all you need for that:

I appreciate your presence, and I hope the tour was enjoyable! I'd be pleased to advise you of any developments about this property. I also spoke with a few other homeowners in the neighborhood today who are thinking about selling their property shortly.

I'd love to keep in touch with you and let you know as soon as any new properties are available before they hit the market.

You know, in such a competitive market, getting updates early might be helpful.

This script makes your client know that there is a realtor he or she can lean on when he or she needs information about real estate. You might just have succeeded in winning them to your side.

BONUS #6

EFFECTIVE FOLLOW UP METHOD & SCRIPTS FOR REALTORS

Following up with the SMS

As a real estate agent, if you haven't thought about utilizing text messaging to engage with your prospects, let me call your attention to an intriguing fact.

The National Association of Realtors survey indicated that 62% of all home purchasers prefer their realtor to communicate property details through text message.

But shockingly, just an estimated 5% of realtors presently converse via text.

There's no dispute that texting will make your conversations speedier and more efficient.

But texts are significantly different from other communication channels since they have a character restriction and demand you to explain your argument in brief.

Therefore, establishing the correct messaging for this channel will take considerable consideration. In this piece, we'll go through various real estate SMS Scripts that you may use as inspiration to construct your own messages.

Well, the good news is that you don't have to be the best writer to develop a successful text message script. With a little coaching, anyone can compose a superb SMS to captivate their audience. The real estate text scripts that we'll go through will supply you with that guidance that might be the golden piece for you. Here is a blockbuster buyer script example.

Hi Paul, this is Agent Bob of Evan's real estate firm and I am looking forward to talking with you about your home search. I will try calling as soon as I can, but in the meantime, are there any homes you want to take a look at?

A seller can also be convinced by typing something like

Hi Paul, this is Bob working for Evans brokerage. Thanks for reaching out about your lead magnet . I'm excited to help you. I'll be sending your lead magnet within the next 24 hours to your email.

It is important to send the next text immediately after the previous one.

I would also love to schedule a quick 10- to 15-minute meeting to explain what's going on in the market right now. Is 4pm on Friday good for you? Or would 3pm on Saturday be better?

Following Up using the Email

Whether you've just shown a potential buyer around the most expensive property on your books or you're trying to pursue a sequential property flipper, when this comes to real estate, a strong follow-up email game may be worth millions of dollars.

Buyers are becoming progressively younger, and that indicates they are increasingly choosing online contact rather than phone conversations or face-to-face encounters.

So while realtors pride themselves on their interpersonal skills as well as on property knowledge, nowadays it's just as necessary to be excellent at communicating using email.

To develop captivating email copy that establishes lasting relationships with your real estate prospective customers, you have to customize it and make it relevant to them. This will make them feel that you know their exact desires. you must finally conclude with a call to action.

If you're dazzled by all of this, don't worry; we've got you covered; you can make your email stand out by utilizing our email script, like this one. Mr Paul still remains our outstanding sample client in these scripts.

A buyer script can go like this

Hello, Mr Paul,

I'm checking in to see whether you received the listing information I provided you last *Monday.*

I'd love to hear your thoughts on the properties I've posted. Did any of these capture your attention? Or are they lacking key characteristics that you're seeking in your new home? If that's the case, I'd like to provide you with information concerning some of the other fantastic properties on my list.

As always, I'd be delighted to schedule a meeting with you in order to view any homes that interest you.

Please do not hesitate to contact us if you have any comments or questions about any of the properties.

Thank you very much.
Bob

Fantastic! This is a way to make a buyer become interested in your properties.

A seller might require something like this.

Hello Paul,

Thank you so much for taking the time on Friday to discuss the prospective sale of your house - it was a pleasure to meet you!

To validate some of the information you provided, you have a timeframe to sell your house and feel it is worth roughly $2000000. Is this still true?

The following stage will be for me to develop a bespoke valuation report, which I will give by the end of the week. Do you have time next week to discuss the report?

In the meanwhile, if you have any queries or issues, please do not hesitate to contact us.

Thank you very much.
Bob

Research reveals that 44% of agents lose up and cease sending emails after one "no," and 22% give up after two "no's." That indicates that two-thirds of realtors never follow up an additional time, which means they might be losing a lot of business deals. These scripts can assist you in getting started with your email journey.

Following up with phone outreach.

We can all acknowledge that 'follow-up caller' is one of our least preferred hats to wear as real estate salespeople.

However, you should know what is most essential to them from the initial chat since this will impact what you say in your follow-up conversations. It is impossible to overstate the importance of taking precise notes throughout your calls in order to prepare for a follow-up session.

Because you employ a range of outreach tactics, you will want a script for follow-up calls. This script will show you how to perform these follow-up calls flawlessly, and for illustration purposes. Mr Paul still remains our sample client and Bob remains our smart sample real estate agent.

Here is a conversation between a real estate agent and his client. This is to simulate how a phone outreach should look like to be perfect.

Agent Bob: Hello, Paul, this is Bob from Evan's real estate. We last spoke on Friday and I am checking in to see if you had any questions or if there was anything else I could do for you.

Paul: Not at all. We had a setback, and it appears that we will be unable to do anything for some months.

Agent Bob: Oh, I understand, and the last thing I want to do is annoy you. How can I assist you right now? Can I help you with anything?

Paul: Not at all.

Agent Bob: Do you want to continue receiving email alerts?

Paul: Well, I don't want to trouble you since I'm not sure when we'll be ready now.

Agent Bob: It is not at all bothersome. I want to make sure I'm available when you are. Let me ask you a question. Can I check in to see how things are going? I don't care when or if you decide to buy— what matters to me is that you are content where you are and that things happen when it is convenient for you. I'll tell you what—I'll return in two weeks to say hello. No need to worry. I want to stay in touch with you.

We have also simulated a script on how phone outreach can help sellers believe in your expertise

Hello Paul, my name is Bob, and I work for Evan's real estate firm. How are you doing?

I am following up with you following our last conversation to see if you're ready to accept a cash offer on your house.

Do you require any additional information from me? Is the timeframe I mentioned suitable for your needs? Can we arrange for me to visit the property? Ok. When and where are you available?

Perfect! I'll email you the specifics later today. I'll look forward to meeting you on.

I know what you are thinking. What if they didn't answer the phone?

Then you may convey your message via voicemail and ensure not to go straight to the point after a brief introduction.

Hello, Paul. My name is Bob, a real estate agent from Evan's real estate firm. You mentioned that you want to sell your house when we chatted last week. I just wanted to check in and see how things were doing. **If you know the client well enough, you can also add information that your client might find intriguing . You might say something like** *'Do you know that you can get your dream house in Minnesota at almost the same price of your current house?*

So that is it!... Now you know what to say and write to your clients when you want to follow them up on their decisions.

If you want more highly effectively follow-up script, go to https://soldouthouses.com/followup to get our done-for-you follow-up script

CONCLUSION

Thank you for taking the time to read this book. It has been a passion of mine for years to share the information I have grown as an agent. Your job, is to take what I have written, read through it one or two more times so you have the information committed to your memory and then go out and start getting your feet wet. Start with small deals and see what happens.

The more you practice the better your results will become over time. Also, remember, you never have bad deals, you simply have learning experiences. Not taking it personally when a deal falls through or going galactic when you get that first commission check will help keep you grounded and in the game.

The world of real estate is a long one. Take your time, find the right deals for you, and start building something that you can be proud of.

And if need more resources and tips on how to grow your real estate business, go to https://soldouthouses.com/ to learn more about our products, books & services.

Let's get started.

ABOUT THE AUTHOR

Who Am I?

Hi, my name is Nick Tsai. I'm a digital marketing expert, and I have over 10 years of marketing experience.

Ten years ago, I was a realtor. As a rookie, I struggled to get clients even though I followed the traditional advice from the industry:

- Distributing flyers
- Posting classified ads
- Cold calling
- Cold mailing

But nothing worked for me.

I was frustrated, tired of struggling, and hopeless. I worked 12-hour days, every day and still got no clients. I eventually burned out and quit. I lost my confidence and self-doubt crept in.

Those were the worst days of my life.

Then one day, I received a phone call that changed everything.

It was from a stranger who wanted me to help him sell this house.

I had never called him, never mailed him, and didn't even know who he was.

But, for some reason, he found my website.

It was an ugly blog I used as a personal notebook where I wrote down everything I learned about real estate.

For some strange reason, it became the #1 ranking real estate blog in my local area.

In the next few months, people kept calling. They asked me questions about real estate and even begged to be taken on as clients.

All of a sudden, I became the go-to expert in the local area.

And getting clients became effortless.

It was an "aha" moment for me and

I realized, "It's easier to attract clients than to chase clients."

In the past, I pursued potential clients by cold calling, cold mailing, and sending flyers (aka junk mail). I became an annoying salesperson.

But by harnessing the power of the internet, I can easily reach people who are ready to buy and can position myself as an expert!

So, I decided to dive into internet marketing to discover how I could attract more clients online. I studied countless marketing books, attended marketing seminars, and learned from the best marketing experts in the world.

And that's why I set up Soldouthouses.com so realtors like I once was can get results with digital marketing.

Be sure to visit https://Soldouthouses.com and discover all the real estate marketing tools & templates and follow our youtube channel at https://youtube.com/@soldouthouses

233

Be sure to visit https://Soldouthouses.com and discover all the real estate marketing tools & templates and follow our youtube channel at https://youtube.com/@soldouthouses

RESOURCES

Thanks for taking this book; the following are some resources that can help you take your real estate business to the next level

1. The Ultimate Real Estate Marketing Checklist (Free)

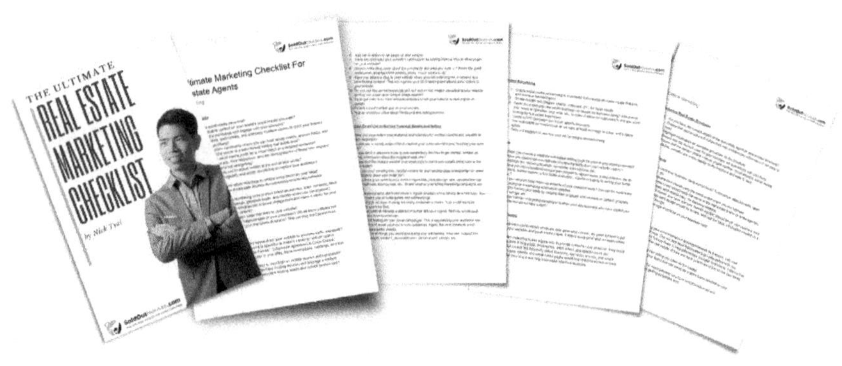

Get 86 proven real estate marketing ideas to
generate more leads online

please go to https://soldouthouses.com/checklist
to download your free checklist

2. Sold Out Houses Pro Membership

You can also join our pro membership to get access to over 1700+ real estate marketing tools & templates for only a few bucks a day.

Go to https://soldouthouses.com/pro/
to learn more about this special package

3. Our Digital Marketing Services

Want my team to take care of your internet marketing for you?

Visit Our site at https://services.soldouthouses.com/ to see what you can do to bring your real estate marketing to the next level

4. 150 done-for-you real estate infographics

Get your social media content ready in the next few minutes.

You can get your infographic package at https://soldouthouses.com/infographics.

5. 360 real estate social media post templates

Create professional social media content
quickly with those templates

You can get those templates at

https://soldouthouses.com/socialmediaposttemplates

6.360 real estate ad templates

Create professional social media ad images
quickly with those templates

You can get all templates at
https://soldouthouses.com/adtemplates

7. Easy Real Estate Funnels (Done-for-you website & funnel templates)

Want to have a professional real estate website? get our done-for-you website and funnel template and get your website up and running quickly

Learn more at https://soldouthouses.com/easyfunnel

8 10X Leadgen Masterclass

Discover how to generate more leads with digital marketing ,
Sign up Here At https://soldouthouses.com/masterclass

www.ingramcontent.com/pod-product-compliance
Lightning Source LLC
La Vergne TN
LVHW011919060726
842528LV00010B/1689